University of California - Davis

Davis, California

Written by Tristen Chang
Edited by Adam Burns and Jessica Pecsenye

Additional contributions by Omid Gohari,
Christina Koshzow, Chris Mason, Joey Rahimi,
Jon Skindzier, Luke Skurman, Tim Williams, Sylvette Sein,
and Sara Ginsburg

ISBN # 1-59658-141-7
ISSN # 1552-0889
© Copyright 2005 College Prowler
All Rights Reserved
Printed in the U.S.A.
www.collegeprowler.com

Special thanks to Babs Carryer, Andy Hannah, LaunchCyte, Tim O'Brien, Bob Sehlinger, Thomas Emerson, Andrew Skurman, Barbara Skurman, Bert Mann, Dave Lehman, Daniel Fayock, Chris Babyak, The Donald H. Jones Center for Entrepreneurship, Terry Slease, Jerry McGinnis, Bill Ecenberger, Idie McGinty, Kyle Russell, Jacque Zaremba, Larry Winderbaum, Paul Kelly, Roland Allen, Jon Reider, Team Evankovich, Julie Fenstermaker, Lauren Varacalli, Abu Noaman, Jason Putorti, Mark Exler, Daniel Steinmeyer, Jared Cohon, Gabriela Oates, Tri Ad Litho, David Koegler, Glen Meakem, and **the UC Davis Bounce Back Team**.

College Prowler™
5001 Baum Blvd.
Suite 456
Pittsburgh, PA 15213

Phone: (412) 697-1390, 1(800) 290-2682
Fax: (412) 697-1396, 1(800) 772-4972
E-mail: info@collegeprowler.com
Website: www.collegeprowler.com

Welcome to College Prowler™

During the writing of College Prowler's guidebooks, we felt it was critical that our content was unbiased and unaffiliated with any college or university. We think it's important that our readers get honest information and a realistic impression of the student opinions on any campus — that's why if any aspect of a particular school is terrible, we (unlike a campus brochure) intend to publish it. While we do keep an eye out for the occasional extremist — the cheerleader or the cynic — we take pride in letting the students tell it like it is. We strive to create a book that's as representative as possible of each particular campus. Our books cover both the good and the bad, and whether the survey responses point to recurring trends or a variation in opinion, these sentiments are directly and proportionally expressed through our guides.

College Prowler guidebooks are in the hands of students throughout the entire process of their creation. Because you can't make student-written guides without the students, we have students at each campus who help write, randomly survey their peers, edit, layout, and perform accuracy checks on every book that we publish. From the very beginning, student writers gather the most up-to-date stats, facts, and inside information on their colleges. They fill each section with student quotes and summarize the findings in editorial reviews. In addition, each school receives a collection of letter grades (A through F) that reflect student opinion and help to represent contentment, prominence, or satisfaction for each of our 20 specific categories. Just as in grade school, the higher the mark the more content, more prominent, or more satisfied the students are with the particular category.

Once a book is written, additional students serve as editors and check for accuracy even more extensively. Our bounce-back team — a group of randomly selected students who have no involvement with the project — are asked to read over the material in order to help ensure that the book accurately expresses every aspect of the university and its students. This same process is applied to the 200-plus schools College Prowler currently covers. Each book is the result of endless student contributions, hundreds of pages of research and writing, and countless hours of hard work. All of this has led to the creation of a student information network that stretches across the nation to every school that we cover. It's no easy accomplishment, but it's the reason that our guides are such a great resource.

When reading our books and looking at our grades, keep in mind that every college is different and that the students who make up each school are not uniform — as a result, it is important to assess schools on a case-by-case basis. Because it's impossible to summarize an entire school with a single number or description, each book provides a dialogue, not a decision, that's made up of 20 different topics and hundreds of student quotes. In the end, we hope that this guide will serve as a valuable tool in your college selection process. Enjoy!

OMID GOHARI ◯ CHRISTINA KOSHZOW ◯ CHRIS MASON ◯ JOEY RAHIMI ◯ LUKE SKURMAN ◯
The College Prowler™ Team

UNIVERSITY OF CALIFORNIA, DAVIS

Table of Contents

Introduction from the Author

When I tell people I'm going to college at UC Davis, they usually do a little double take. "Really?" they'll ask incredulously, "Wow. Study hard." I hardly ever know how to respond to that, so I just flash my best "Oh-I'm-trying-to" smile and wait for their approving nod to excuse me from the conversation. Often, it looks like my school spirit is missing in action; but this is hardly the case. I am a die-hard Aggie fan. However, when confronted with the school's stellar academics, I usually shrug it off. Sure, I know Davis is ranked as one of the top ten public schools in the nation. And yes, I feel incredibly privileged to be here. However, that is not what makes me so proud of my current Aggie status. The satisfaction I have in pulling on my UC Davis sweatshirt, flashing my student ID, and even giving out my campus e-mail address has little to do with Davis' world-renowned degree programs. The pride I have in my school is founded more on the principles of community that distinguish Davis from so many other institutions.

It's not hard to find people familiar with UC Davis. Known for its science programs with a history rooted in academic excellence, and many of the top degree programs in the country; Davis is inherently a well-known campus. At least, the academics are well-known. What many people don't know about Davis are the very things that many students most cherish: the stimulating atmosphere, the supportive and encouraging professors, and the diverse, amicable student body.

While most consider Davis a "nerd school" and picture the students as snooty intellectuals, that is far from the case. Surprisingly, Davis has an overwhelmingly friendly campus . . . most people just don't know about it.

I hope that in reading this book you catch a glimpse of the aspects of Davis that so many students hold dear. I'm not throwing out numbers or rankings or advertising the campus; chances are, if you're interested in Davis, you've already heard them anyway. But there are so many other elements that contribute to this dynamic school, and many are indescribable. I love being able to cart my books to the Quad and study for hours in the sunshine. I love looking up from my Chem lab in the Silo and being able to ask the stranger next to me for help. I love riding my bike home from work, passing a rugby game, and being invited to join. I love the Arboredum, the trees, the bikes, I even love the cows. There is so much more to Davis than just Genetics and Veterinary Medicine, and I hope this book provides some insight into the real scene: what life is really like at the University of California at Davis.

Tristen Chang, Author
UC Davis

By the Numbers

General Information

University of California, Davis
One Shields Avenue
Davis, California 95616

Control:
Public

Academic Calendar:
Quarter

Religious Affiliation:
None

Founded:
1908

Website:
www.ucdavis.edu

Main Phone:
(530) 752-1011

Admissions Phone:
(530) 752-2971

Student Body

Full-Time Undergraduates:
20,962

Part time Undergraduates:
2,510

Full-Time Male Undergraduates:
10,346

Full-Time Female Undergraduates:
13,126

Female:Male Ratio
55.9%:44.1%

Admissions

Overall Acceptance Rate:
60%

Regular Acceptance Rate:
60%

Total Applicants:
32,506

Total Acceptances:
19,367

Freshman Enrollment:
4,786

Yield (% of admitted students who actually enroll):
24.7%

Early Decision Available?
No

Early Action Available?
No

Regular Decision Deadline:
November 30

Regular Decision Notification:
March 31

Must-Reply-By Date:
May 1

Transfer Applications Received:
6,853

Transfer Students Accepted:
4,139

Transfer Students Enrolled:
1,761

Transfer Acceptance Rate:
42.5%

Common Application Accepted?
No

Supplemental Forms?
None

Admissions Phone:
(530) 752-2971

Admissions E-mail:
undergradadmissions@ucdavis.edu

Admissions Website:
www.ucdavis.edu

First-Year Students Submitting SAT Scores:
SAT I Range (25th – 75th Percentile):
1080 – 1300

SAT I Verbal Range (25th – 75th Percentile):
510 – 630

SAT I Math Range (25th – 75th Percentile):
570 – 670

Retention Rate:
98.6%

Top 10% of High School Class:
95%

Application Fee:
$40

Financial Information

Tuition:
$6,351 in-state
$23,307 out-of-state

Room and Board:
$10,234

Books and Supplies:
$1,414

**Average Need-Based
Financial Aid Package**
(including loans, work-study,
grants, and other sources):
$9,864

**Students Who Applied For
Financial Aid:**
60%

**Students Who Applied For
Financial Aid and Received It:**
47%

**Financial Aid Forms
Deadline:**
March 3

Financial Aid Phone:
(530) 752-6667

Financial Aid E-mail:
undergradfinaid@ucdavis.edu

Financial Aid Website:
faoman.ucdavis.edu

Academics

The Lowdown On...
Academics

Degrees Awarded:
Bachelor
Master
Doctorate

Most Popular Areas of Study:
(7%) agricultural business and management
(7%) psychology
(5%) biology/biological sciences
(5%) communication studies/ speech communication and rhetoric
(5%) economics

Undergraduate Schools:
College of Letters and Science
College of Engineering
College of Agricultural and Environmental Sciences
Division of Biological Sciences (part of Letters and Science)

Full-Time Faculty:
1,392

→

Faculty with Terminal Degree:
98%

Student-to-Faculty Ratio:
19:1

Average Course Load:
13-15 units (4 classes)

4 Year Graudation Rate:
51%

5 Year Graudation Rate:
77%

6Year Graudation Rate:
81%

Special Degree Options

Accelerated Program, Cross Registration, Double Major, Dual Enrollment, English as a Second Language, Honors Program, Independent Study, Internships, Student- Designed Major, Study Abroad, Teaching Credential

AP Test Score Requirements

Possible credit for scores of 3 and higher

IB Test Score Requirements

Possible credit for scores of 5 and higher

Sample Academic Clubs:

English Honors Program, Model United Nations, Astronomy Club, Society of Women Engineers, AIDS Education Project

Best Places to Study:

The Quad

Arboredum

Shields Library

Did You Know?

The Gourman Report ranks UC Davis **number one in the nation** for its programs in Veterinary Medicine, Plant Biology, and Genetics.

- UC Davis is the national leader for Ph.D. graduates of **Biological Sciences**.

- Two UC Davis centers—for Fuel Cell Vehicles and Hybrid Drivetrains—have been named as **U.S. Department of Energy (DOE) National Centers** within the DOE's Centers of Automotive Technology Excellence program. Their research goal is to develop advanced vehicle power systems. These power systems will spur U.S. automotive research and manufacturing and help solve pressing air-pollution and global-warming problems.

- A particle accelerator developed by **Tom Cahill, a UC Davis professor** of atmospheric science, is being used to track air quality at more than fifty national parks, monuments and wilderness areas. The technology has already helped reduce smog in the Grand Canyon and has been applied in California to measure air quality problems and find solutions to smog in the Lake Tahoe Basin and the Central Valley.

- Statistician **David Rocke**, professor in the Graduate School of Management and the School of Medicine's department of epidemiology and preventive medicine, is helping the U.S. Environmental Protection Agency to improve the accuracy of very low-level measurements of water pollutants and to develop computer software to conduct the measurements. The project, funded by the EPA, has created a breakthrough model being adopted by industry nationally as a voluntary standard for examining water and wastewater.

Students Speak Out On...
Academics

"**The professors are very helpful and approachable. They are always there if you need help just as long as you remember to ask. The classes can vary greatly: from keeping you on the edge of your seat to having you fast asleep from sheer boredom.**"

Q **"The teachers at UC Davis are nice for the most part.** A little hard to get in contact with unless you want to work at it. Basically, office hours are the only time to do this. Classes are only interesting if you pick interesting classes. It's that simple: if you take Calculus, it's not going to be interesting, whereas Human Sexuality might be a little different. But school is school no matter where you go; it's all hard work."

Q **"Most lecturers are pretty cool and laid back**; however, I'm not a science or engineering major. For those who are, they would probably complain about thick accents and stubborn professors and TAs. Although as a Psych major, I've never had problems with bad TAs or professors."

Q "I have had some really good teachers and some really bad teachers; I think it's pretty common anywhere you go. But I have greatly enjoyed my Animal Science classes. They were informative and very interesting. I looked forward to attending them every week. **If anyone wants to become a vet, Davis is the place to be.** Besides being the top vet school in the country, the animal science teachers are excellent."

Q "**All classes are really hard, and I think the teachers vary, depending on the class.** Some of my classes I found to be quite boring because the teacher was not that great. The course material was not that bad, but the teacher would just lecture the whole time. However, I did have some really good teachers, which would make the class very interesting and worthwhile."

Q "The worst thing about Davis is that **you go from getting As in high school math to flunking** the 21-series math."

Q "**Most of my classes have had 200-plus students**, so I have never really gotten to know many teachers."

Q "At first the sheer size of the lecture halls kind of freaked me out; it was like going to class in a football stadium. But after the first week, I just sat up front and didn't even notice the 400 other people behind me. There is a good side to it too: **if you want to leave class, you just get up and go, and nobody has to notice.**"

Q "I'm sure that most of the teachers are really smart and educated in their fields, but sometimes **the thick accents make it hard to understand them.** The material is hard enough to understand without the added difficulty of deciphering every word they say. However, I have always found that they're willing to work individually with me after class, and that has been really helpful."

Q "The teachers here are generally pretty laid-back and very approachable I've noticed. **They usually really encourage their students to come in during their office hours, which is very helpful.** You always hear those horror stories of professors being these imposing devilish figures complete with horns, and well, that's not the case here. Some professors are strict, yes, but almost all are willing to help their students."

Q **"I was a little intimidated by the 500-person lecture hall.** Chem 194 seemed like a stadium. I didn't know how my professor would ever get to know me. Luckily, I had an amazing Chem professor: he made himself available outside of class for office hours, e-mailed me answers to my panicked 4 a.m. study-session questions, and he actually knew my name by the third week of the quarter."

Q "Profs are most helpful if you talk to them one-on-one, especially after class, on your own time, or their office hours. Outside of class, **it's really easy to get to know them."**

Q "Classes are tolerable. **They can have you questioning your sanity around finals, but they're pretty cool.** I recommend taking a P.E. class each quarter because they're fun and don't count in your GPA. Also, take some English classes; they usually have pretty hot women."

The College Prowler Take On...
Academics

With more than 110 undergraduate fields of study, Davis has the greatest academic diversity of all the UC campuses. This gives students the chance to take classes that interest them, and the majority of students seem to appreciate the opportunities that Davis presents. However, the large lecture halls intimidate some students and make it harder to develop personal relationships with professors. Strangely, this kind of attention isn't uncommon: if you want your professors to know you, they will be more than willing to do so. You have to take the initiative, though. Still, there's something to be said for anonymity when you can sneak out the back door of lecture without the professor knowing who you are.

Despite the challenges encountered by some, most students seemed satisfied with their courses. They commended the professors and appreciated their willingness to offer further explanations of course material. The majority of students expressed a genuine interest in their classes, recognizing the professors' expertise and valuing their friendliness. Students do, however, express frustration in dealing with thick accents of TAs and challenging course material. On the other hand, though, challenging course material is only expected at an institute of higher learning. This is not to be mistaken as high school – you will definitely have to be more independent, and, without a doubt, have to work much harder.

The College Prowler™ Grade on
Academics: B

A high Academics grade generally indicates that professors are knowledgeable, accessible, and genuinely interested in their students' welfare. Other determining factors include class size, how well professors communicate, and whether or not classes are engaging.

Local Atmosphere

The Lowdown On...
Local Atmosphere

Region:
Northern California

City, State:
Davis, California

Setting:
Suburban

Distance from Sacramento:
20-30 minutes

Distance from San Francisco:
60-90 minutes

Points of Interest:
Lake Tahoe
American River
Clear Lake
Napa and Sonoma Valleys
Cache Creek
Dillon's Beach

Closest Shopping Malls:

Arden Fair Mall- Sacramento
Downtown Plaza- Sacramento
K Street Mall- Sacramento
County Fair Mall- Woodland

Closest Movie Theatres:

Signature Theatre- Davis
(617) 734-2501

Major Sports Teams:

Sacramento Kings (NBA)
Sacramento Monarchs (WNBA)

City Websites

www.city.davis.ca.us/downtown/profile.cfm
www.davisdowntown.com

Did You Know?

Four Fun Facts about Davis:

1. Davis was **originally Davisville** 1868-1917 until the railroad put it on the map, and (so the story goes) the name was shortened to save on printing costs.

2. Davis has the **highest number of bikes** per capita in all America.

3. Every Wednesday from April to September, the **Farmers Market** hosts live music to serenade the shoppers.

4. A portion of the Arboredum is dedicated to **Dr. Ruth Storer**, the first practicing female physician in Yolo County.

Local Slang

Hella - very, a lot: ("Davis is hella cool; there's hella cows here!")

Dry - alcohol free ("I've been dry all quarter.")

Tree huggers - environmental activists ("There are a lot of tree huggers.")

Students Speak Out On...
Local Atmosphere

"I love the atmosphere in Davis. It is such a great college town and all the people are very friendly. No, I don't think other universities are present. Definitely visit the Farmers Market on Saturday mornings and Wednesday. That is so much fun. There are no places I would stay away from."

Q "**Davis is a great college town.** Everything revolves around the university, which makes things really easy. College students provide the supply and demand of this economy. There are no other universities in Davis, but there are a few community colleges near by and a few state schools as well. UC Berkley is probably the closest university. I would recommend just experiencing as much of Davis as humanly possible."

Q "It's a definite college town; **everything seems to be catered to the students.** The food and movies are reasonably priced and being able to get to Sac and San Fran so easily makes it so there's lots to do."

Q "Davis is unique. We are way more liberal than the surrounding areas. Sacramento is to the east, and we make fun of their campus a lot. Woodland is a farming area so not much is there besides Wal-Mart and Target, which is good for cheap college students. Don't go to West Sacramento; it's sketchy. Davis is small. **Your entertainment depends on you and your friends, which aren't too hard to come by here.**"

Q "Davis is quite the college town. **I definitely suggest trying the many wonderful eating establishments.** There may not be much else to do (there is an under ground bowling alley, for all you bowling fans), but the restaurants are great."

Q **"The town is cool and laid back, but it's small and there's not a whole lot to do**; then again, I come from LA so sometimes it seems like I'm living in a barn."

Q "The atmosphere is awesome. **People are open-minded and laid-back.** You don't get snooty intellectuals the way you would at say, Stanford. Yuck."

Q **"The atmosphere is great because you live in a suburb, so everybody is laid back and relaxed.** Yet at the same time there's always something to do even if it means driving fifteen minutes to Sacramento, you're bound to have a good time. If you have never been to Davis, you should definitely visit the animal science area as the school is known for being the best vet school in the world. It's also a good idea to visit Woodstock's pizza as it is one of the social centers of the town."

Q **"Don't come to Davis if you're lazy.** First off, you'll flunk out of school, and second, your social life will suffer. Here, parties don't come to you; you go to them. If you get up and get out, Davis has a lot to offer, but if you expect an invitation from the clubs, chances are you'll spend a lot of time sitting around by yourself complaining that there's nothing to do in this town. Also, don't come if you're lazy because the women seem to like really driven guys, so you'd strike out there too."

Q "Davis is a very small town—that's probably the first thing you should know about Davis. **It's not for big city kids.** It's very laid-back, very friendly, and very open. I found it really refreshing, coming from the Los Angeles area myself. I love the atmosphere here."

Q "The downtown area is home to quaint little coffee shops and restaurants, and the whole town has that nice, small town feel to it. **The town's covered in parks and bike paths, making it a great outdoor town, as well as a very environmentally-conscious town."**

The College Prowler Take On...
Local Atmosphere

UCD students have no problem admitting that Davis isn't the most bustling university. In fact, that's one of the things they most appreciate. Although entertainment is limited in a small suburban setting, students seemed grateful for the relaxing environment after a stressful day spent over the books. Because the town is essentially built around the university, students enjoy the convenience of a college town and the comfortable atmosphere of a community. Davis is also just a car ride away from Sacramento, San Francisco, Tahoe, and Cache Creek. It's close enough to the beach to throw together a full-day adventure or even a weekend camping trip.

The majority of students expressed overwhelming satisfaction with the local atmosphere. Although some complained about the lack of entertainment, others claimed that all it takes to have fun in town is a little creativity. Students who prefer the hum of metropolitan life will undoubtedly appreciate Davis' close proximity to Sacramento and San Francisco, but it's important to keep in mind the fact that the town of Davis itself is far from fast-paced. If students are flexible and able to make their own fun, this small town may fit just right. You have to be creative.

The College Prowler™ Grade on

Local Atmosphere: B

A high Local Atmosphere grade indicates that the area surrounding campus is safe and scenic. Other factors include nearby attractions, proximity to other schools, and the town's attitude toward students

Safety & Security

The Lowdown On...
Safety & Security

Number of UCD Police:
51

UCD Police Phone:
(530) 752-3289

Safety Services:
Campus Violence Protection
Program

Escort Service

Tipsy Taxi

Self-defense classes

ASUCD Walking Escorts

Health Services:
Emergencies/ Urgent Care

Primary Care

Women's Clinic

Men's Health

Specialty Care

Dietitian Assessment

Mental Health

Clinical Support Services

Health Center Office Hours

School Year:

Monday-Friday (except Wednesday): 8 a.m.-7:30 p.m.

Wednesday: 9 a.m.-7:30 p.m.

Weekends: 9:30 a.m.-1 p.m. (Urgent Care only)

Summer Session/Breaks:

Monday-Friday (except Wednesday): 8 a.m.-5 p.m.

Wednesday: 9 a.m.-5 p.m.

Closed University holidays

Did You Know?

ASUCD, the **largest student-run organization in the nation**, runs a free escort service that will pick up and drop off students free of charge.

Students Speak Out On...
Safety & Security

"The campus is definitely a place where you can feel secure while still not feeling oppressed by overbearing security. Thanks to student-run programs such as the Student Escort Service and Tipsy Taxi, there is always help when you need it."

Q "Davis is incredibly safe; and other than people stealing bikes, **I can't think of any huge safety issues on campus."**

Q "Campus is pretty safe, and **there is always the escort service** to take you around if you are afraid to go somewhere."

Q "Safety on campus is good. **There is a campus cruiser that will pick up students late at night, which is very helpful.** There is also Tipsy Taxi that takes students to and from parties on the weekends, which is also a very safe and helpful service."

Q **"I think that Davis is the safest UC school** compared to UCLA or UC Berkeley. The town is basically a college town, so I think that that is why it is so safe. Let me put it this way—the number one crime in Davis is bike theft."

Q "I know our security looks really bad because of the attacks we had early this year, but it could have happened anywhere, and now, because of those unfortunate events, **there is a huge movement to increase the campus security."**

Q **"Davis is very safe.** It's one of the things I enjoy most about living here. I am originally from Los Angeles, and it is great being able to leave my front door unlocked without worrying about who or what is going to drift into my house. I always feel safe in Davis, even when I am walking around at night. The town is extremely centered on the university, so it's pretty safe."

Q "There is a group called the Cal Aggie Hosts who will escort you around campus at night. Generally the campus is pretty safe. In my time here, I have not heard of any problems. **Campus police patrol from time to time,** and I would say that the worst thing that could happen is getting your bike stolen. It happens because of the sheer amount of bikes on campus. Other than that, it is safe on campus, even at night."

Q "Security and safety is pretty good. **There are cops everywhere, all the time,** not because there are a lot of crimes but because they don't have anything to do in this little peaceful town."

Q "On-campus security and safety are pretty decent on campus. **There's always ways to call for help if need be**, and the whole campus, which is huge, is very well-lit, even in the remote areas."

Q **"There's an on-request after-hours escort service** to help students get to their dorms safely after it gets dark."

Q **"Of course no campus is 100% safe**, but I'm proud to say that you won't have to worry about violence or other crimes in general."

Q **"It's safe here.** Security is everywhere. Just don't walk alone at night, and you're guaranteed to keep safe. However, I know people that do walk alone at night, and nothing bad has ever happened to them."

Q **"Davis feels really safe**, but it is always a good idea to have a buddy after dark."

The College Prowler Take On...
Safety & Security

Most Davis students feel they have to worry more about locking their bikes than their front doors. Students express feelings of security, probably credible to Davis' small suburban setting. Most students are familiar with the services offered by the school, though many hardly feel the need to use them. They feel comfortable enough to walk alone at night, although that is not an advisable thing to do. Despite the fact that UC Davis seems safe enough, there is still a huge effort currently striving to increase security on campus. You can never be too safe.

UC Davis funds a free escort service that starts running every night at 6 p.m., there are self defense classes on campus, and plenty of campus safety phones. Students are still advised to carry a bike light or flashlight though. Davis has some great trees, but they also make for some dark areas on campus. There are plans to install more lights in those areas and on the bike paths, but having your own light is still a good idea. Despite the darkness, there is little need to panic; in a town where the biggest crime problem is bike theft, safety isn't too much of an issue.

A

The College Prowler™ Grade on

Safety & Security: A

A high grade in Safety & Security means that students generally feel safe, campus police are visible, blue-light phones and escort services are readily available, and safety precautions are not overly necessary.

Computers

The Lowdown On...
Computers

High-Speed Network?
Yes

Wireless Network?
Yes

Number of Labs:
15

Numbers of Computers:
650

Biggest and Busiest Labs:
Library
Bookstore
MU

Other Labs:
Language Labs (A, B, C, D)
Learning Resource Centers
Cuarto-Emerson
Cuarto-Castilian
Tercero
Segundo
Primero

24-Hour Labs

No, but hours are extended during finals.

Charge to Print?

In the computer labs, students are allotted 200 printed pages per quarter (they don't roll over), and for everything after that, it costs 10 cents a page

Did You Know?

Davis has one of the **highest student-computer ratios** in the nation, with over 97% of students owning their own computers

Students Speak Out On...
Computers

"There are a ton of computer labs, and they don't really get crowded—maybe a little towards the end of the semester when term papers are due, but the ones in the dorms are a safe bet."

"**The University now requires students to have access to their own computer** so having your own computer is obviously a must. The network is fast and easy to use, although at certain times it can become crowded. It is best to access computers in buildings other than the library or bookstore, seeing as both of those locations are always the most crowded."

"**I would definitely recommend bringing a computer,** there is no way to survive without one. And I've never been in a computer lab, or a library for that matter. Is that surprising?"

"Well **starting this year they make you bring one anyway;** it's not really an option."

"Computer labs tend to be pretty crowded so I would definitely recommend bringing your own computer. It's also annoying to be in line for the labs and see people doing everything on the computers because theirs is broken or something. **I try and use the labs just for printing.**"

"You have to bring our own computer anyway, and **computer labs can be crowded**—it depends on when you go."

Q "Yes, definitely bring your own computer. I would feel lost without my own computer. **I never really used the computer labs**, only a few times when my computer was broken. It was not too crowded when I went, but it is still a lot easier to have your own computer."

Q "In the dorms, **the network is pretty good.** It's really fast, and it's free. We use a lot of e-mail here between professors for class, and we register for classes online. Plus, it's a pain to use someone else's. If you have to use the computer labs on campus, it's not a big deal. The first 200 pages you print are free."

Q "There are computers available in labs. They get busy but not ridiculously so. I have a computer at home but I usually print on campus. It's not a problem. **There are several labs, half have Macs and the others have PCs.** The network is great; everyone gets broadband Internet access."

Q "You should definitely bring your own computer. I've generally noticed **the computer labs to be quite crowded**, and I know in fact that the university itself advises all incoming students to have a computer of their own."

Q **"The university offers financial aid to students who express need in purchasing a computer**, though, which is quite helpful. Believe me, for the amount of work you'll be doing on a computer for your classes, it's in your own best interest to purchase one, or at least have one with you."

Q "The computer **network is probably the fastest I've ever seen.** It's a T3 connection if you live in the dorms and use the computers on campus. The computer labs are never crowded (except around finals) because there are plenty of computers for everyone."

The College Prowler Take On...
Computers

Davis actually requires that incoming students bring their own computers, and financial aid is available to help them do so. The professors do a lot of communicating via the Internet, and there are lots of course related e-mails, websites, and notes that get distributed daily. Some courses even have online quizzes and midterms, downloadable lecture notes, and practice exams that can only be completed by using a computer. Most students see this as convenient, and also a way to stay abreast of the modern technology. However, it is a change from the classical textbook/lecture style of teaching that most students experience in high school. College not only opens the doors of the social and academic world; it encourages and enhances the application of technology. With the stellar network that the University offers, computers definitely play a key role in education at UC Davis; a role that is only secondary to the professors.

Although students are required to have their own computers, there are also computer labs on campus; but students mainly use them to quickly check their e-mail or to print. Each student gets 200 free printed pages per quarter at the computer labs. Many students take advantage of the printing labs, and rightly so. Students should be forewarned that the lines can get pretty long during finals week when everyone is printing their research paper. If you have a paper due and do not have a printer, you should get it finished a day or two before it's due for the sheer fact that waiting in line to print it could cause a late paper. This goes against what has become a sort of universal mentality for college students everywhere: procrastination. However, if you have your own printer, you can procrastinate all you want.

B-

The College Prowler™ Grade on
Computers: B-

A high grade in Computers designates that computer labs are available, the computer network is easily accessible, and the campus' computing technology is up-to-date.

Facilities

The Lowdown On...
Facilities

Student Center:
The MU is the main student center, but campus is home to many: the Cross Cultural Center, Women's Center, and LGBT, just to name a few.

Athletic Center:
The Rec Hall

Rec Pool

ARC

Popular Places to Chill:
The Silo

The Arboredum

The Quad

The Coffeehouse

The MU Courtyard

Libraries: (7)
Shields Library

Women's Center Library

Agricultural and Resource Economics Library

Law Library

Loren D. Carlson Health Sciences Library

Physical Sciences and Engineering Library

UCDMC Library

Campus Size in Acres:
5,200 acres

Did you know?

The Robert and Margrit Mondavi Center for the Performing Arts features the state-of-the-art 1,800-seat Jackson Hall, a 250-seat Studio Theatre, a grand lobby, reception rooms, and a landscaped entry plaza. A part of the UC Davis campus, **Mondavi Center** stems from the legacy of UC Davis Presents—the leading presenter of world-class performing arts in the Sacramento region for nearly 50 years.

What Is There to Do On Campus?

Enjoy the live bands that play in the Quad

Study or take a stroll in the Arboredum

Work out at the Rec Hall, Rec Pool, or ARC

Meet up with friends for lunch at the Coffeehouse

Use your meal plan at the Silo

Take a breather in the MU courtyard or student lounge

Enjoy the art at the MU gallery

Grab some people for a game of Frisbee in the Quad

Check out the merchants outside the Bookstore

Go bowling at the MU alley

Study or nap in the Quad

Play air-hockey or pool in the underground gaming area

Sunbathe on the Quad

Movie Theatre on Campus?

Kindof- Chem 194 shows occasional movies on campus

Bar on Campus?

No

Coffeehouse on Campus?

Yes, and it is appropriately named The Coffeehouse

Bowling on Campus?

Yes, at the MU

Students Speak Out On...
Facilities

"Shields Library is the best library ever! It's quiet when it needs to be, but you can also take friends there to study with."

Q "Everything at Davis is really good and easily accessed. **The Rec Hall is a great place to work out.**"

Q "The **facilities on campus are all very up-to-date and nice.** The computers are all top of the line Macs so you can run into some problems if you own a PC. The athletics facilities are very nice as you would expect from a school that has won the Sears Cup most of the last few years."

Q "I just can't say enough about the facilities here. **UC Davis' recreation hall is one of my favorite places to go, as well as the Quad.** These places are usually crowded because people are always up for staying in shape and basically unwinding under the sun. The Shields Library is state-of-the-art and that's the only place I can get my work done because dorm life is so distracting!"

Q **"The Recreation Hall is free entry for students**; it has basketball courts, racquetball, weights machines and free weights, a track, a rock climbing wall, and different aerobic classes, such as hip-hop, step, abs, butts & guts, kickboxing, and yoga. The Memorial Union (MU) has the bookstore, a study lounge, and a student-run coffeehouse that has a ton of tables in and around it for eating, studying, and napping. The library's really good too. It's huge, so if you need to hide from a grouchy roommate, go there. If you need a book they almost definitely have it."

Q **"I love the ARC . . . I want to live there.** Seriously, it looks like a hotel with work-out equipment instead of beds. I just wish the dance studio had windows instead of walls so I could enjoy the ballerinas! Err, I mean ballet."

Q "We have an awesome Recreation Center, a **great health center, great computer labs—UCD takes good care of us."**

Q **"We have a large array of student facilities on campus.** We have this really huge recreation hall that's open almost all the time, with tons of athletic equipment, a pool, and even a rock-climbing wall. They hold some classes there as well. There is also a game area, equipped with pool tables and even a full-length bowling alley."

Q "The only facility I really used was the Rec Hall. **The Rec Hall was nice and big**, and they are building an even nicer gym that is supposed to be ready soon."

Q "Pretty nice, **the Rec Hall is lame but they're building a new one."**

The College Prowler Take On...
Facilities

Overall, students seem very impressed with the facilities on campus. As if the current facilities aren't enough, this year, Davis is constructing a new Rec Hall, aquatic center, and dormitory. They are starting work on the new student health center, too. Most students rave about the campus Recreation Center (fondly referred to as the Rec Hall), the student union (MU), computer labs, and libraries. Besides being pleased with the quality of the facilities, students are also grateful for the accessibility. The options are there and plentiful, and students are nothing but satisfied.

While UC Davis students enjoy many top-notch facilities, one establishment is particularly renowned. The Shields Library is one of the largest libraries, nationwide. It provides a place for students to study (alone or with a study group), cram for midterms, and, of course, sleep. With 3.24 million library volumes, Shields is a priceless resource for students to utilize for both academic reasons and leisurely reading.

The College Prowler™ Grade on
Facilities: A-

A high Facilities grade indicates that the campus is aesthetically pleasing and well-maintained; facilities are state-of-the-art, and libraries are exceptional. Other determining factors include the quality of both athletic and student centers and an abundance of things to do on campus.

Campus Dining

The Lowdown On...
Campus Dining

Freshman Meal Plan Requirement?
Yes

Meal Plan Average Cost:
$2000

Places to Grab a Bite with Your Meal Plan:

Brennan's Coffee
Location: The Silo

Food: Coffee shop and bakery

Favorite Dish: Cappuccino and blueberry muffin

Hours: Monday- Friday 10 a.m.-9 p.m.

Cafe Fresca
Location: The Silo
Food: Sandwiches, sushi, wraps
Favorite Dish: Chicken Ceasar Wrap
Hours: Monday- Friday 10 a.m.-9 p.m.

Carl's Jr.
Location: The Silo
Food: Fast Food
Favorite Dish: Criss-cut fries
Hours: Monday- Friday 10 a.m.-9 p.m.

→

La Crepe
Location: The Silo

Food: French

Favorite Dish: Fresh Strawberry Crepe

Hours: Monday- Friday 10 a.m.-9 p.m.

Pizza Hut
Location: The Silo

Food: Pizza

Favorite Dish:

Supreme Pizza

Hours: Monday- Friday 10 a.m.-9 p.m.

Stock Pot
Location: The Silo
Food: Soup and Sandwiches

Favorite Dish: Old Fashioned Turkey Noodle Soup with Wheat Bread

Hours: Monday- Friday 10 a.m.-9 p.m.

Sub City
Location: The Silo
Food: Sandwiches
Favorite Dish: Vegetarian Sandwich

Hours: Monday- Friday 10 a.m.-9 p.m.

Taco Bell Express
Location: The Silo

Food: Fast Food

Favorite Dish: Chicken soft taco

Hours: Monday- Friday 10 a.m.-9 p.m.

Off-Campus Places to Use Your Meal Plan
None

24-Hour On-Campus Eating?
No

Other Options:
Dining Commons- Tercero is hands down the best DC on campus

Student Favorites
The Silo and the MU

Did You Know?

UC Davis **professor Pam Ronald** genetically engineered rice—the food staple for many areas of the world—to resist a major bacterial disease. Her 1995 discovery is part of an effort to develop strategies to boost global rice productivity while decreasing agricultural chemical use, particularly in Third World nations.

Students Speak Out On...
Campus Dining

"The food on campus is very good. There is fast food for those who are in a hurry, but there's also a cafeteria and dining commons. As long as you remember that it's a good idea to vary where you eat, you won't get annoyed with the food."

Q **"I would recommend exploring off-campus food.** I have three words for the dining halls: Horrible Crap Meals. No, they aren't really that bad, however, they get old fast."

Q "I love the dining halls! **They have an awesome variety of food, and the staff is so nice.** I work at the Coffee House on campus, which I think is a great place to eat. There's also the silo for the junk food types out there. Definitely purchase Munch Money so you don't have to pay at the Silo."

Q "The food on campus depends on whether or not you are a picky eater. Personally, I am a very healthy eater and sometimes I do not like everything that is offered at the dining commons. But, there is always something I could eat. **The salad bar at the dining commons is great, and there are quesadilla makers and a grill that I like.** Frozen yogurt is always there too. There is always pizza and cereal. There are plenty of food options at the DC, it just depends if you like all the food they offer. The silo is a great place to eat on campus. Lots of good food is offered there. There is also food at the Memorial Union, but I never ate there because it costs money. At the silo I would use my Munch Money so it wouldn't cost me anything!"

Q **"The Silo is definitely the spo**t; you run into everyone you know there. Munch Money is also a good idea; all you do is swipe your card and you're good to go. But the dinning halls on the other hand are a whole other story. If you like your food with a side of grease, that's the place to go!"

Q "Food on campus is pretty good. There's The Silo, which has fast food places as well as food like crepes and sandwiches. There's **the Memorial Union coffee house, where you can get burritos, bagels, and salads.** I lived in the Tercero dorms last year and I think they have the best DC food compared to the other."

Q **"The food on campus is not bad at all.** If you are going to be a freshman, you will be living in the dorms, and the DCs (dining commons) are pretty good. I must say that off-campus food is a lot better, but it all depends on your style. We have the typical fast food joints that none of us can stay away from, plus Jamba Juice and Plutos, a great salad place. They are located in Downtown Davis."

Q **"On-campus food is decent.** We have two places to go eat. The CoffeeHouse (or CoHo) is actually the largest restaurant in northern California and is run by ASUCD. It's like a very large cafeteria. There's every kind of food you can think of. Across campus from that there's the Silo, which has Taco Bell, Carl's Jr., Subway, a crepe place (crepes are huge in Davis), and some other fast food places."

Q "Your first year here you will most likely stay in the dorms to eat. **Dorm food is nutritious but I found myself eating chicken sandwiches, fries, and side salad for dinner all too often.** Memorial Union has a student run food court, which is also an option. Here you can find pizza or burritos, soups, salads, or entire meals."

The College Prowler Take On...
Campus Dining

Students seemed satisfied with the food on campus, but feel that there is still much to be desired. The Silo is popular with basics such as Taco Bell, Carl's Jr., and Pizza Hut, plus Stock Pot soups, Sub City sandwiches, Crepeville, and Café Fresca salads, sushi, parfaits, wraps, and sandwiches. And, only in Davis will you find organic frozen food meals, and those are also available at the Silo. Students also rave about the convenience of Munch Money—prepaid dollars on their student account that allows them to swipe meals at the Silo—and recommend it as a convenient addition to any meal plan.

The dorm food is, well, dorm food. Students seem less than impressed, but find the dining commons convenient and with a plethora of options. For the unadventurous DC diner, cereal, salad, and the sandwich bar may prove to be dietary staples. The dining commons have plenty of vegetarian and vegan selections, and some "Theme Nights" (Luau night, Caribbean Night, etc.) that students seem to enjoy. Whatever the Dining Commons (commonly referred to as the 'DC') lacks in its entrees, it makes up with its desserts . . . the frozen yogurt is a popular favorite, and with at least five desserts to choose from every night, Davis students always end their meals on a good note.

The College Prowler™ Grade on
Campus Dining: B

Our grade on Campus Dining addresses the quality of both school-owned dining halls and independent on-campus restaurants as well as the price, availability, and variety of food.

Off-Campus Dining

The Lowdown On...
Off-Campus Dining

Restaurant Prowler:
Popular Places to Eat!

Caffe Italia
Food: Italian
1121 Richards Blvd., Davis
(530) 758-7200
$10- $15 a person
Mon.-Sun. 11 a.m.-10 p.m.

Cafe Bernardos
Food: California/ Light Cuisine
234 D St., Davis
(530) 750-5101
$15-$20 per person
Mon.-Sat. 11:30 a.m.-2 p.m.;
5 p.m.-10 p.m., Sun. 4 p.m.-9 p.m.

Chipotle Mexican Grill
Food: Mexican
227 E St., Davis
(530) 758-3599

Cool Features: Build your own burritos and tacos between $5 and 10 a person
Mon.-Sat. 10 a.m.-10 p.m.,
Sun. 11 a.m.-10 p.m.

→

Crepeville

Food: French

330 Third St. Davis

(530) 750-2400

$10 and under a person

Sun.-Thu. 11 a.m.-9 p.m., Fri.-Sat. 11 a.m.-10 p.m.

The Davis Graduate (The Grad)

Food: Italian, pizza, grill

805 Russell Blvd. Davis

(530) 758-4723

Cool Features: Dancing, bar, foam parties

$10 and under a person

Mon.-Sun. 11 a.m.-2 a.m.

Dos Coyotes Border Cafe

Food: Mexican

North Davis: 1411 W. Covell Blvd.

South Davis: 2191 Cowell Blvd.

North Davis: (530) 753-0922

South Davis: (530) 758-1400

$10 and under a person

Mon.-Sun. 11 a.m.-10 p.m.

El Mariachi Taqueria

Food: Mexican

400 G St., Davis

(530) 750-0688

$10 and under a person

Mon.-Sun. 11 a.m.-10 p.m.

Fuji Chef

Food: Japanese

213 G St., Davis

(530) 753-3888

Cool Features: Sushi buffet under $10 a person for menu orders, under $15 for sushi buffet

Mon.-Sat. 11:30 a.m.-2 p.m;. 5 p.m.-10 p.m., Sun. 4 p.m.-9 p.m.

Fusions Asian Bistro

Food: Thai

2171 Cowell Blvd. Suite F Davis

(530) 297-7100

$15 and under a person

Mon.-Sat. 11:30 a.m.-2 p.m., 5 p.m.-10 p.m., Sun. 4 p.m.-9 p.m.

Fuzio

Food: California/ Light Cuisine

500 1st St. #11, Davis

(530) 753-3877

Cool Features: Candlelit outdoor patio

$10 and under per person

Mon.-Sun. 11 a.m.-10 p.m.

Hibachi Grill

Food: Japananese

403 Third Street, Davis

(530) 758-1505

$10 and under a person

Mon.-Sun. 11 a.m.-10 p.m.

Hoa Viet Restaurant

Food: Vietnamese

303 First St. Davis

(530) 759-9888

$10 and under a person

Mon.-Sat. 10:30 a.m.-9:30 p.m. Closed Sun.s.

House of Chang

Food: Chinese

2151 Cowell Blvd., Suite C Davis

(530) 758-3988

$10 and under a person

Mon.-Sun. 11 a.m.-10 p.m.

Kathmandu Kitchen

Food: Indian/ Middle Eastern Cuisine

234 G St., Davis

(530) 756-3507

$10 and under a person

Mon.-Sun. 11 a.m.-10 p.m.

Noodle Express

Food: Chinese

301 G St., Davis

(530) 753-7755

$5 to $10 a person

Mon.-Sun. 11 a.m.-10 p.m.

Pluto's

Food: California/ Light Cuisine

500 First St., Davis

(530) 758-8676

Pluto's (continued....)

Cool Features: Outdoor patio, buffet style eating under $10 a person

Mon.-Sun. 11 a.m.-10 p.m.

Silver Dragon

Food: Chinese

335 F St., Davis

(530) 758-1318

$5 to $10 a person

Mon.-Sun. 11 a.m.-10 p.m.

Sophia's Thai Kitchen

Food: Thai

129 E St., Davis

(530) 758-4333

Cool Fact: First Thai restaurant in Davis

$10 and under a person

Mon.-Sat. 11:30 a.m.-2 p.m.; 5 p.m.-10 p.m., Sun. 4 p.m.-9 p.m.

Super Salad

Food: California/ Light Cuisine

620 Fourth St., Davis

(530) 753-7300

$10 and under a person

Mon.-Sun. 11 a.m.-10 p.m.

Thai Recipes

Food: Thai

132 E St. Suite 1H/G Davis

(530)759-2099

$10 and under a person

Sun.-Thu. 11 a.m.-1 a.m., Fri.-Sat. 11 a.m.-2 a.m.

Tokio Restaurant

Food: Japanese

620 N. Covell Blvd., Suite 105, Davis

(530) 758-4560

Cool Features: Sushi bar, Mongolian barbeque

$10 and under, excluding sushi bar

Sun.-Thu. 11 a.m.-1 a.m., Fri.-Sat. 11 a.m.-2 a.m.

Sam's Mediterranean Cuisine

Food: Mediterranean

247 Third St. Davis

(530) 758-2855

$10 and under a person

Mon.-Sun. 11 a.m.-10 p.m.

Steve's Place Pizza

Food: Pizza

505 L St., Davis

(530) 758-2800

$15 and up per pizza

Mon.-Fri. 11:30 a.m.-10 p.m., Sat.-Sun. 11:30 a.m.-11 p.m.

Strings Italian Cafe

Food: Italian

1411 W Covell Blvd. #1, Davis

(530) 753-1313

$15 and under a person

Mon.-Sun. 11 a.m.-9 p.m.

Woodstocks Pizza

Food: Pizza

219 G Street, Davis

(530) 757-2525

Cool Features: Delivery to dorms

$10 and up per pizza

Mon.-Thu. 11 a.m.-10 p.m., Fri. 11 a.m.-12 a.m., Sat. 4 p.m.-10 p.m.

Late-Night, Half-Price Food Specials:

Noah's Bagels "day old" specials

Closest Grocery Stores:

Nugget Market

1414 E. Covell Blvd., Davis

Safeway

1451 W. Covell Blvd.Davis,

(530) 757-4540

2121 Cowell Blvd., Davis-Phone: (530) 792-8500

24-Hour Eating

Jack in the Box

Best Pizza:

Woodstock's Pizza

Best Chinese:

Noodle Express

Best Breakfast:

Crepeville

Best Wings:

G Street Pub

Best Healthy:

Plutos

Best Place to Take Your Parents:

Caffe Italia

Did You Know?

On campus there is the **Experimental College Garden** that students can use to grow their own produce.

Students Speak Out On...
Off-Campus Dining

> **"Plutos, Fuzios, Crepeville, Farmers Market . . . there are so many places! I've been here two years and I still haven't been to them all."**

○ "There are **many options for food off campus so I recommend it.** Davis has a very diverse atmosphere."

○ **"The restaurants off campus are good as long as you're not looking for authentic Mexican food.** If you're looking for Asian food you won't have too look far and you can definitely find food in your price range. I would recommend Cafe Italia, Woodstock's Pizza, and Noodle Express."

○ "The restaurants off campus are great. **So many options! Plutos is a great place and is very popular.** Sophia's Thai Restaurant is also really good. There are so many places to eat, like Delta Venus, Crepeville, or Cafe Bernardo's."

○ "Davis doesn't really have many chain restaurants. You won't find Denny's or Applebee's or anything like that, though we do have a Baker's Square. **The best thing about the restaurants here is that they're so unique.** Plutos is my personal favorite—the way it works there is you get this little punch card and move through the buffet lines, and they punch all the items you get and ring you up at the end. It's great, especially when you're just getting off work and only have three bucks in your wallet."

Q **"The restaurants here are sweet!** I've heard that we're known for Asian food but there is a ton of other stuff too—I love the Mexican food here. Dos Coyotes and Chipotle are affordable, and I always have plenty of leftovers to take home."

Q "The food is wonderful. **Only in Davis will you find restaurants that have poetry readings, live music, dancing, foam parties, and such ethnically diverse food.** Delta of Venus is good food and they kind of cater to vegetarians and vegans. Taqueria Quadalajara—the best Mexican food this side of the border—is great. Sophia's is an awesome Thai restaurant. They even have this special room where you take off your shoes and kneel on pillows and eat off of a short table."

Q "I work downtown and there is this city ordinance that was passed to try and keep small businesses alive in Davis . . . so there are a lot of family-owned places. There are over 350 small businesses here, and, while it's kind of a drag that there's no Target or Wal-Mart, all the restaurants make up for it, and you can easily get to Woodland for the convenience items. **The Davis restaurants are so unique and of such a high caliber,** I'm so glad that downtown isn't swarming with dime-a-dozen places like Denny's, where the quality rivals crap."

Q "Great Wall of China, Fuzio's, Sophia's Thai, Woodstock's . . . **Davis has some great food**, but if you want real Mexican food and Chipotle isn't quite cutting it, go to Woodland. It's a ten-minute drive or bus ride (not the most convenient thing ever) but it is so worth it."

The College Prowler Take On...
Off-Campus Dining

The off campus restaurants fare well with Davis students. Some even claim that the dining establishments are some of the best things about the town! An advantage of the college-town arrangement is low-priced food, and students seem to take advantage of the bargains whenever possible. With ethnically diverse options including Italian, Indian, Mediterranean, Asian, Mexican, French, and contemporary California cuisine, downtown Davis provides students with nearly as many culinary options as a more metropolitan city.

Despite Davis' small size, students have no problem finding palate-pleasing meals off campus. Restaurants are authentic and unique, ranging from the dollar menu at In-N-Out Burger to the more upscale establishments like Soga's and String's. Overall, students seem to enjoy the downtown area, and are always able to find a decent meal.

B

The College Prowler™ Grade on
Off-Campus
Dining: B

A high off-campus dining grade implies that off-campus restaurants are affordable, accessible, and worth visiting. Other factors include the variety of cuisine and the availability of alternative options (vegetarian, vegan, Kosher, etc.).

Campus Housing

The Lowdown On...
Campus Housing

Room Types:
Single
Double
Triple
Suite

Best Dorms:
Cuarto- Castilian

Worst Dorms:
Segundo- Regan Hall

Dormitory Residences:
Primero Area: Laurel and Manzanita Halls
Floors: 3
Total Occupancy: 300
Bathrooms: Private
Co-Ed: Yes

Primero (continued...)
Room Types: Studio, One, Two, Three, and Four bedroom apartments
Special Features: All apartments are furnished, carpeted, air conditioned, and include laundry facilities.

Segundo Area: Malcolm, Ryerson, Bixby, and Gilmore Halls
Floors: 5
Total Occupancy: 800
Bathrooms: Communal
Co-Ed: Yes
Room Types: Single, Double
Special Features: Specialty programs: Health Science, Science, and Quiet Program

→

Segundo Area: Regan Hall

Floors: 2

Total Occupancy: 400

Bathrooms: Communal

Co-Ed: Both co-ed and single sex floors

Room Types: Single, Double, Quad

Special Features: Specialty Programs: International Relations, Multiethnic program, Music, Arts, and Performance program, Davis Honors Challenge, Quiet program.

Tercero Area: Lysle Leach Hall

Floors: 1

Total Occupancy: 178

Bathrooms: shared between 4-5 rooms

Co-Ed: Yes

Room Types: Single

Special Features: Nearby convenience store

Tercero Area: Pierce and Thille Halls

Floors: 3

Total Occupancy: 12 buildings, housing 70 students each

Bathrooms: Communal

Co-Ed: Yes, with the exception of one all-women building

Room Types: Single, Double, Triple, Plaza Suite, and Quad Configuration

Special Features: Casa Cuauhtemoc, Wellness/Substance-Free Community, Asian Pacific American Theme House, all women's building

Cuarto Area: Thoreau Hall

Floors: 3

Total Occupancy: 225

Bathrooms: One per suite

Co-Ed: Yes

Room Types: Ten-person suites, Two Double and Two Triple rooms per suite

Special Features: All units are air-conditioned and carpeted. Specialty program: Outdoor Experience

Cuarto Area: Webster, Emerson, and Castilian Halls

Floors: 3

Total Occupancy: 1200

Bathrooms: Semi-private

Co-Ed: Yes

Room Types: Single, Double, and Triple rooms in suites of four, five, and six occupants

Special Features: The halls are furnished, air conditioned, and have access to pools and hot tubs. Specialty program: Outdoor Experience

Undergrads on Campus:

27%

Number of Dormitories:

23

Number of University-Owned Apartments:

3

Bed Type:

Twin or Extra Long Twin

Available for Rent:

Nothing

Cleaning Service?

No

You Get:

(In the dorms) A twin bed, a desk, chair, dresser, lamp, shelves, and trash can

Also Available:

Furnished on campus apartments

Did You Know?

In an attempt to help students live with like-minded people, Davis has developed "specialty programs" that **groups students of common interests in the same dorm**. There are more than ten specialty programs, ranging from Outdoor Experience to the Quite Program, Music Arts and Performance to the Health Sciences. Students select their specialty programs separately from their dorm choices, and the programs have priority. For example, if you state that you wish to participate in the International Relations program (located in Regan Hall) but want to live in the Cuarto dorms, you will most likely be assigned to Regan Hall. This is important to keep in mind when filling out your housing papers.

Students Speak Out On...
Campus Housing

{ **"The dorms are okay. I recommend the off-campus suites, a.k.a. Cuarto. I would hate to be cooped up in one room all day."**

Q **"The dorms are great and a good place to meet roommates for the rest of your academic career.** The best dorms on campus are Primero Groove and the Cuarto area. But keep in mind that if you go for Primero Groove and don't get it, you're usually moved to the back of the list on other dorms and put up in Regan, the worst dorm on campus."

Q **"Cuarto rocks!** It allows privacy, but at the same time you can meet people just as easily in traditional dorms. They're also more spacious and give you a better feel of life after dorms."

Q "Cuarto all the way baby! . . . **The suites are great, but you have to be willing to lose the traditional college dorm life for luxury."**

Q "My dorm experience was wonderful. **I lived in the off-campus suites and was very much spoiled.** I had my own sink, lots of shelves, a huge walk in closet, and a nice-sized room. The off campus suites are very, very nice. But, it is definitely a different experience than the on-campus dorms. If you want the traditional college experience, then go for the on-campus dorms. I would say put Segundo as your first choice if you want that kind of experience. Stay away from Regan and Tercero. They are on-campus dorms as well, but not as nice as Segundo. If you want a very nice, spoiled kind of experience, than put Cuarto as your first choice."

Q **"Cuarto, especially Castillian is the best!** Your own bathroom and living room make it more like home while still creating the dorm atmosphere. Steer clear of Tercero unless you really like the smell of cows."

Q "Cuarto was fun, but **I hear Regan sucks."**

The College Prowler Take On...
Campus Housing

Students realize that the most important aspects of dorm life are not which ones are nice and new but in the way the dorms are set up. Segundo is designed in a typical dorm style, with one room and anywhere from one to three people living in it. The rooms are not carpeted and residents use communal bathrooms, but with that setup, students usually get to know everyone on their floor and make a lot of new friends. Tercero is set up similarly, but the buildings are in close proximity to the cows and some complain about the smell. Still, students point out that Tercero has a significantly better DC, so it's a trade off. Cuarto and Primero are set up suite-style, and are more like apartments. Primero suites have their own kitchens, and are, by far, the nicest, but students claim those dorms don't seem to be as social. Cuarto has suites that house anywhere from five to ten people, they are carpeted, and have control over the central heat and air. They also have their own bathrooms, which are nice, but students are expected to clean them and supply the toilet paper.

Davis dorms are set up differently to accommodate students' different living styles, and picking a favorite just depends on what's important to you. If you want to live in the lap of luxury but not really have the most happening social life, choose Primero. If you want to meet a ton of people in typical dorm style, Segundo may work for you. If you want to meet a ton of people, eat much better food than the rest of the freshmen, and don't mind when windy days blow 'eau de cow' in your direction, pick Tercero. If you want to make a few close friends and a lot of acquaintances, a small suite in Cuarto would probably work well. If you're aiming to make a ton of really close friends, but not too many acquaintances, a big suite in Cuarto would probably suit you well. No matter what though, students agree that the dorms provide a once-in-a-lifetime experience that no student should miss

The College Prowler™ Grade on

Campus Housing: C-

A high Campus Housing grade indicates that dorms are clean, well-maintained, and spacious. Other determining factors include variety of dorms, proximity to classes, and social atmosphere.

Off-Campus Housing

The Lowdown On...
Off-Campus Housing

Undergrads in Off-Campus Housing:

73%

Average Rent for a Studio:

$550- $750 per month

Average Rent for a 1BR:

$600- $800 per month

Average Rent for a 2BR:

$1,000- $1,300 per month

Popular Areas:

South Davis

Downtown Davis

For Assistance Contact:
Web:

www.housing.ucdavis.edu

Phone: (530) 752-1990

E-mail: webmaster@mailbag.
housing.ucdavis.edu

Students Speak Out On...
Off-Campus Housing

"The housing off campus is very convenient especially with the university supplying busses to almost all off-campus housing. As long as you keep on top of your utilities, it is definitely worth it."

Q "Yes, **go with off-campus housing.** It's the only way to go."

Q **"The great thing about living off campus is that you're suddenly exposed to a whole new world of house parties.** No longer are you a little freshman limited to the madness of the frat houses, but you can throw your own stuff, and hear about lots of other parties in nearby apartment complexes."

Q "I work in student government, and we are really focusing on housing. It is becoming a big problem. **We currently still have a vacancy rate, but it's below one percent.** So after your first year, you will be able to find a place, but it'll probably be expensive—about $400 a month."

Q **"Housing off campus is extremely convenient unless you're living really far away!** Our buses run all over the city so, it's totally easy to live off campus and still be able to do stuff. I think because Davis is such a small town and so based on the university that housing off campus has to be convenient! There is not enough housing on campus because the university is accepting more students than the city can handle! This problem should get better because they are building a lot of new buildings."

Q "Housing is decent. You can find a place to live if you have friends you want to live with. **There are some expensive places but they are nice as well.** I don't think you will find dumps, so to speak, but there are some cheap places as well. This town is huge on biking so you can just ride your bike into town."

Q "There really is no choice—**housing is pretty hard to get past freshman year, but there are lots of places to choose from in Davis, apartment-wise.** Don't be too closed minded about budgeting though or you may never find a place."

Q "Living off campus is nice, but you may find yourself starting to miss the DC; yes, the very same DC that had you gagging freshman year. **Doing your own dishes sucks, and for most guys, eating your own cooking sucks worse.**"

Q **"Housing after freshman year is definitely worth it.** It is going to be very nice to live in an apartment and be away from the dorms. I did love the dorms a lot, but it will be very nice to live in an apartment."

Q "It's a lot cheaper to live off campus, but finding an apartment is a huge pain. **The vacancy rate here is something like 0.8%, so don't count on getting into your first choice.** And if you're bent on getting a certain apartment, be prepared to fight for it—we camped out for nineteen hours in the apartment lobby to get on a waiting list for ours! It sounds outrageous (and it totally is), but now that we have it, it was all worth it."

Q "Though cheaper than the dorms, **housing is still expensive.** We have a four-bedroom place and three of us pay $500, $505, and $510 for our own rooms. One girl pays $570, but she's in the master and has her own bathroom."

Q "Let's just say that they don't call it the 'Davis Housing Crisis' for nothing."

Q **"Dorms are good the first year,** but after that, get an apartment."

The College Prowler Take On...
Off-Campus Housing

Admittedly, Davis housing is less than easy to find. With a vacancy rate hovering under one percent, students are frustrated with the lack of openings and the high prices. However, despite these factors, most second-year students opt to live off campus rather than return to the dorms, and end up saving money by doing so.

Because of Davis' convenient size and bus system, students are free to live anywhere in the city. They enjoy free transportation and a housing department geared towards helping them find off-campus housing that suites their needs, and many appreciate the luxuries. Generally, students seemed content with the housing situation; and agreed that, if started early enough, a search for housing will likely end in a choice apartment.

The College Prowler™ Grade on

Off-Campus Housing: B+

A high grade in Off-Campus Housing indicates that apartments are of high quality, close to campus, affordable, and easy to secure.

Diversity

The Lowdown On...
Diversity

Asian or Pacific Islander:
43.6%

White:
43.02%

Hispanic:
10%

African American:
2.58%

American Indian:
0.8%

International:
4.28

Unknown:
6.9%

Out of State:
3.19%

Most Popular Religions:
There are several Christian groups and Asian American religious groups, but most religious activities are held off campus.

Political Activity

Davis is known for its liberal, politically active campus. The bulletin boards are often papered with flyers inviting students to participate in various protests . . . often, the protests are for conflicting interests.

Gay Tolerance

The campus is very accepting of its gay students, and even hosts "Gay Pride Day" in June. The LGBT (Lesbian Gay Bisexual Transgender) is a student center on campus that targets the interests and needs of the gay community. Though the campus is very open-minded, the gay community is not overwhelmingly vocal.

Economic Status

Being a major university, UCD has students from very diverse economic backgrounds. Because the campus is so laid back, differences in socioeconomics are barely noticeable, with the majority of students appearing to have come from middle-class backgrounds. More than half of Davis students receive some form of financial aid, so economics play a minimal role in campus life.

Minority Clubs

African-American Health Sciences Association, Asian Law Students Association, Asian Student Union, Black Law Students Association, Chicano/Latino Medical Students Association, Chinese American Student Association, Cross-Culture Coalition, Filipino Americans in Medicine, Hmong Student Union, LaRaza Student Association, Masala, Mga Kapatid, Mujeres Ayudando LaRaza, NaKeikio Hawaii Nei, Native American Law Student Association, Pan-African Student Association, United Filipino-American Student Association

Did You Know?

UC Davis ranked in the top eight schools nationwide for number of **degrees awarded to students of underrepresented ethnic groups**.

Students Speak Out On...
Diffusity

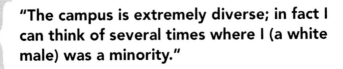

"The campus is extremely diverse; in fact I can think of several times where I (a white male) was a minority."

Q **"Very diverse**, which is expected at universities."

Q "When I got here, my first impression was, 'Wow, I've never seen this many Asian people in one place before.' But my friend down the hall was like, 'Wow, I've never gone to school with this many other white people before.' **It all depends on your point of view, but it's pretty diverse."**

Q "The campus is very diverse. **There are plenty of clubs on campus that you can get involved in.** For example, I'm involved in a Filipino club called FAHC. It's for those involved in health-related careers although you don't necessarily have to be Filipino. I have a couple friends in it who aren't."

Q **"Davis is not as diverse as say Cal or UCLA**, but we have diversity. We have many different cultural weeks, and racial tensions are very little compared to somewhere like NY."

Q "We do pretty well with diversity. **A lot of clubs support the diversity and campus programs as well.** We have organization for socialist, republicans, gay communities, Muslim, Palestinian, Jewish, German club, and a bunch more. I'm impressed by our diversity."

Q "UCD is very pro-diversity. I'm gay, and I've never felt threatened on campus. **There's a definite presence of all minority groups on campus**, and any kind of discrimination is dealt with harshly by the university."

Q "I've heard that **Davis is the most ethnically diverse university of all the UCs**, but that doesn't mean a whole lot to me. I tend to think of diversity in terms of interests and opinions . . . and I see a ton of that here. That's what matters to me."

Q "There is a little diversity in Davis with **the dominant races being Caucasian and Asian.**"

The College Prowler Take On...
Diversity

Davis students are lucky to have such a diverse campus. There are many interest groups run by students and staff, making it easy to get involved with other students of similar interests. There are organizations for different majors (Chemistry Club, Society of Women Engineers, Psychology Honor Society, Seele: the literary magazine, etc.), ethnicities (Third World Forum, La Raza Cultural Days, AIR, ImaginAsian, Black Family, etc.), political affiliations (Davis Republicans, Democratic Party, Liberty's Flame, etc.), interests (S.E.E.D., SCTA, Outdoor Adventures, etc.), and just about everything else.

Overall, students recognized the campus diversity and applauded the liberal community. Students hardly felt threatened by racism, sexism, or prejudice, and credited it to the campus' open-minded student body. Despite the fact that Davis has a reputation of being a bunch of hippie, tree-hugging bikers, the campus is actually pretty diverse. If variety if the spice of life, UCD is always looking for new flavors!

B

The College Prowler™ Grade on
Diversity: B

A high grade in Diversity indicates that ethnic minorities and international students have a notable presence on campus and that students of different economic backgrounds, religious beliefs, and sexual preferences are well-represented.

Guys & Girls

The Lowdown On...
Guys & Girls

Men Undergrads:
10,010

Women Undergrads:
12, 740

Birth Control Available?

Yes. Women who have had an exam with their primary care physician or at Cowell Student Health Center can have birth control prescriptions filled for $ten dollars. The health center offers many different contraceptives: pills, condoms, patches, and the shot

Social Scene:

Davis is known for its friendly, laid back campus. The fraternities and sororities tend to have their own social agendas, but there really is no social hierarchy. Students have no reservation in mixing with crowds of different majors, ethnicities, or social circles. Davis is relatively "clique free," and most people are always eager to make new friends.

Hookups or Relationships?

In the beginning of school, it's not uncommon to see all the freshmen randomly hooking up in an insane dating mob, but that begins to die quickly once the excitement of being "on your own" isn't so new anymore. After a while, students meet people in their classes, at parties, on sports teams or in interest groups, at work, or through other friends; they meet new people every day. Davis is known for its friendly campus, and all it takes to meet someone is a simple glance up from studying, eye contact, and a smile.

Best Place to Meet Guys/Girls:

Being the academic institution that it is, Davis keeps students pretty busy with finals every ten weeks. That said, they still find plenty of time to socialize, and it's not uncommon for students to hook up with someone they meet in class, a study group, or at the library. However, those students who want more of a distinction between their academic and romantic lives won't be too hard pressed- there are plenty of weekend parties that draw crowds of singles.

Dress Code

With Davis' laid-back atmosphere, there really is no dress code. Students dress according to the weather rather than according to the trends and seem to prefer clothes that are easy to bike in. On campus, students can be seen in everything from flip-flops to stilettos to cowboy boots, or whatever else they happen to throw on in the morning. Overall, it's a pretty casual campus . . . jeans and tee shirts are more common sights than polo shirts and slacks. But with Davis' diversity, it's not uncommon to see leather jackets, suspenders, Caesar-style sandals, and long flowing skirts—all in the same outfit.

Did You Know?

Top Three Places to Find Hotties:

1. The Quad
2. Parties
3. Library

Top Places to Hookup:

1. Parties

2. Clubs

3. Class

4. Library

5. House parties

Students Speak Out On...
Guys & Girls

"Nobody really cares here . . . guys don't go up to their friends and say, 'Hey, I met this really hot chick.' It's more like, 'Hey, I met this really awesome girl.' By now people have kind of outgrown the obsession with looks."

Q "Sure **the girls here look good . . . with all the bike riding, it's hard not to.** But the most impressive things are their personalities . . . I know that sounds cliché, but they are all smart and driven here, and super nice."

Q **"The guys on campus are drop-dead sexy** and they have some of the coolest personalities I've ever come in contact with."

Q **"The girls on campus are attractive**, and, as a guy, there is a slightly higher number of girls than guys—so less competition is good."

Q "At the beginning of the year I would have said that the scenery at Davis is below average for the most part, but for some reason **the girls seem to come out of the woodwork in the spring, so just be patient.**"

Q **"I really like the guys here . . . they're obviously smart**, but they're not stuck up. More often than not, they play some sort of sport, so they're in good shape, but that's kind of superficial. All the guys I've talked to have been really nice, friendly, and going somewhere in life."

○ "Guys have it great here; the odds are in their favor. **The girls aren't superficial, and they are great to talk to**; I can't say enough about the women's personalities. These are the girls you could picture yourself marrying. And you don't have to be a Casanova to get a date—most girls here are really open minded, not shallow. They don't even seem to care that we'll all be making bank when we graduate."

○ **"All I have to say is girls plus bikes plus miniskirts equals one great combination."**

○ "The **sorority girls are usually pretty hot in the beginning of the year until they get their beer bellies** . . . and then they all start looking alike, talking alike, acting alike, and they all major in communications."

○ **"I don't think the guys or girls on campus are that great.** Nobody really cares. I wouldn't say the guys are hot. Some of the sorority girls can be hot, but a lot of the girls are not too hot either. How hot people are should not be a determining factor in which school you choose though."

○ **"I think Davis has really hot women.** All that bike riding really pays off!"

○ "The smartest thing I ever did was take a dance class with my roommate. Sure, it wasn't quite our thing and we looked ridiculous, but we got over that. **We were the only guys there, surrounded by beautiful women all wearing leotards . . . it made all the ton dues worth it.** The girls totally called us on it, though; they knew we were just in there to check them out, but they were really cool and some of them even let me take them out."

○ **"Everyone is so nice here!** It's easy to meet people and make friends."

The College Prowler Take On...
Guys & Girls

When asked to describe the girls and guys on campus, it's interesting to note that the majority of Davis students respond with appreciative comments based on personalities. Though many are quick to point out the merits of bike riding and free gym access, they also clarify that the personalities and attitudes of the students far outshine the physical appearances. Many also admit that the campus could be slightly better looking, but no students seemed unsatisfied with what the campus had to offer.

Still, with California weather and an inherently active lifestyle, Davis students are pretty good looking. Students are open minded and friendly, and with such a large student body, you're bound to find someone that interests you.

The College Prowler™ Grade on
Guys: B

A high grade for Guys indicates that the male population on campus is attractive, smart, friendly, and engaging, and that the school has a decent ratio of guys to girls.

The College Prowler™ Grade on
Girls: B+

A high grade for Girls not only implies that the women on campus are attractive, smart, friendly, and engaging, but also that there is a fair ratio of girls to guys.

Athletics

The Lowdown On...
Athletics

Athletic Division:
NCAA Division One-
Exploratory Status

Conference:
CCAA

Men's Teams:
Baseball
Basketball
Cross Country
Diving
Football
Golf
Soccer
Swimming
Tennis
Track and Field
Water Polo
Wrestling

**Women's
Varsity Sports:**
Basketball
Cross Country
Diving
Gymnastics
Lacrosse
Rowing
Soccer
Softball
Swimming
Tennis
Track and Field
Volleyball
Water Polo

Club Sports:
32

Intramurals:
35

Number of Males Playing Varsity Sports:
368

% of Males Playing Varsity Sports:
3%

Number of Females Playing Varsity Sports:
344

% of Females Playing Varsity Sports:
2%

Athletic Fields

Hutchison Field

Dairy Field

Russell Field

Howard Field

Toomey Field

A Street Field

East Field

Solano Field

Tercero Field

School Mascot

Mustang/Aggie

Colors

Scarlet and White

Getting Tickets

Just bring your student ID

Most Popular Sports

Footall, Basketball

Overlooked Teams:

Baseball, Gymnastics

Best Place to Take a Walk

Arboredum

Gyms/Facilities

Hickey Gym

Rec Hall

Did You Know?

Davis has the **most diverse and popular competitive recreation program in the nation**. With over 1,400 participants in 35 different IM sports, and 1,400 participants in 32 club sport offerings, Davis has something for everyone!

- Sixteen Aggie teams advanced to **NCAA championships** in 2000-01, with eleven teams placing in the top ten.

- UC Davis is the **six-time winners of NACDA Directors' Cup** for best Division II program in the nation—more than any other school.

- In the Division I Big West Conference, **we compete against Sister UCs**: Santa Barbara, Irvine, and Riverside, as well as seven other schools.

- Davis was named **best NCAA Division II School** of 2002 by Sports Illustrated.

- We were also the twice-named **best school for women athletes** by Sports Illustrated for Women.

Students Speak Out On...
Athletics

"UC Davis has been a powerhouse in Division II sports over the last decade. The sports programs are big and very good. Although, we will be switching to Division I next season—so there could be a slight shift in sports."

Q "I don't think varsity sports are that big on campus. Maybe **football will get more popular now** that we are a Division I school. I don't know how big IM sports are because I was never involved in any, but I don't think they are that big either."

Q "**IMs are the best.** They're a great way to get involved and meet new people. But to be honest, I went to one football game all year and that was it . . . it doesn't seem like many people go."

Q "Sports are pretty big here, **especially football—it's our pride and joy!** Sporting events are always going on and they are a lot of fun. IM sports are also pretty good, and there are plenty to choose from."

Q "Our varsity teams are fairly good. If you have time, **check out Aggie Packs.** They are crazy, and it's lot of fun to go to the events. Football and basketball are the most popular games to go and watch. IM sports are fairly big. Most people continue to come back with the same team . . . once you start joining IM sports, you sort of get hooked on it, and it's a great form of hanging out too."

Q "Varsity sports are pretty big . . . but **just the main ones like football and basketball**. Baseball is good to watch too. IM sports are great! They have different leagues so you can play in the one for you. Some examples are softball, inner tube water polo, touch football, and then they also have basketball, racquetball, and tennis. There really is a variety."

Q "Sports are pretty big on campus. **Our football, baseball, and basketball teams are really good** and draw lots of people to their games. There are IM sports of all kinds, and you will probably find what you like. Most are co-ed."

Q "The IM program is cool, especially **inner tube water polo**, soccer, and softball."

The College Prowler Take On...
Athletics

Now that Davis is moving to Division One, the varsity sports are getting plenty of attention. Football games draw really big crowds, and the Aggie Pack (the largest run student organization in America) encourages the masses by handing out free shirts, water bottles, and other UCD gear. Some students have voiced concern over the fee increases students have incurred because of the move to Division One, but others argue that with the extra money generated by D1 athletics, the campus will be able to make improvements that benefit the entire student body.

So while varsity sports do enjoy some popularity, the club sports at Davis really have the limelight. In the seven years that the Sears Cup has been awarded to Division II schools, Davis has never finished below second place—placing first in just the last three years, and we also placed first two other years. IM sports are pretty big here too, and anyone can participate. There are the traditional sports like soccer, basketball, and volleyball, but Davis also has some less conventional teams: inner tube water polo, Hapkido, and ballroom dancing. There is a wide range of experience on IM teams, from athletes that have played since they were five, to people that are just looking for a way to stay in shape. It's a great way to try new sports, and it also makes it easy to stay involved in sports you already excel in. Everyone's really friendly, and meeting people is really easy when you're both slamming heads while diving for the same volleyball.

A-

The College Prowler™ Grade on

Athletics: A-

A high grade in Athletics indicates that students have school spirit, that sports programs are respected, that games are well-attended, and that intramurals are a prominent part of student life.

Nightlife

The Lowdown On...
Nightlife

Club Prowler:
Popular Nightlife Spots!

The Davis Graduate
805 Russell Blvd., Davis
(530) 758-4723

Bar Prowler:
Cafe Bernardo
234 D Street, Davis
(530) 489-1111

Cafe California
808 Second Street, Davis
(530) 757- 2766

Cantina del Cabo
139 G Street, Davis
(530) 756-2226

The Davis Graduate
805 Russell Blvd., Davis
(530) 758-4723

Delta of Venus Cafe
122 B Street, Davis
(530) 753-8639

➜

Froggy's Restaurant and Bar
726 Second Street, Davis
(530) 758-7550

G Street Pub
228 G Street, Davis
(530) 758-3154

Hunan Bar and Restaurant
508 Second Street, Davis
(530) 753-5174

Rosita's Cocina
132 E Street, Davis
(530) 758-3207

Soga's
217 E Street, Davis
(530) 757-1733

Sophia's Thai Kitchen
129 E Street, Davis
(530) 758-4333

Sudwerk
2001 Second Street, Davis
(530) 758-8700

Bars Close At:
2 a.m.

Primary Areas with Nightlife:
The Cantina
Froggy's
G Street Pub
The Grad
Soga's

Cheapest Place to Get a Drink:
Dollar Night at Sophia's

Favorite Drinking Games:
Beer Pong
Beer Volleyball
Twister
Kings
Sevens

Student Favorites
The Cantina
G Street Pub
The Graduate (The Grad)
Froggy's

Local Specialties:

Theme nights! The Grad hosts a different theme night every night of the week to spice things up and keep students entertained. Popular

Useful Resources for Nightlife

www.davis411.com

www.downtowndavis.com

www.sacentertainment.com

What to Do if You're Not 21

House parties and frat parties are your main options. The Grad has some eighteen-and-over nights, but, being underage, options are pretty limited.

Students Speak Out On...
Nightlife

"The places to go are The Cantina, G Street Pub, and the Grad. Usually a lot of people go to at least one of those. Even though it seems like there isn't that much to do in Davis, you can usually find something. In a town with 26,000 students, there is always something to do."

Q "This is the area in which the campus has a downside. There are a couple of clubs, bars, and other hang out spots (The Graduate, G Street Pub, Froggy's, and Woodstock's Pizza) but it is limited. The school is working on it though."

Q "The Grad is popular, however I only went once for a foam party . . . but it was so fun!"

Q "Bars and clubs are a lot better in San Francisco (of course), but the joints here aren't too bad. Most of us go to The Graduate. It is a restaurant by day and a club/bar at night. Wednesday nights are college nights, and Friday nights are twenty-one-and-over. There [are] couple of other bars in downtown Davis, so bar hopping is within walking distance."

Q "Davis has four bars, three of which are located on the same street. Sacramento is only fifteen to twenty minutes away and has a bunch of good clubs and bars (Polyester, The Rage, and 815 Street are my favorites). San Francisco is about an hour and half away and has a good night life."

Q "**There really isn't a whole lot to do here bar wise**, but there is entertainment to be found. You just have to be flexible and open minded."

Q "In Davis, **we have a really good club called the Grad**; it also has some good food. Most people on go on Wednesday or Thursday because that is the good music night. The other nights are salsa or country. We have many bars in Davis; the most popular are the Cantina and Sudwerks."

Q "There are no real clubs or bars to get excited about. The Grad is fairly entertaining. I go there Salsa night (Thursdays). **Most students don't depend on downtown Davis for entertainment, yet we remain entertained.**"

Q "**There is a good selection of bars but nothing compared to a larger city.** Going to Sacramento for clubs and bars would be your best bet, and it is not that far way."

Q "The bars are a huge scene in Davis. This is especially true from the Greek point of view. T**here isn't much to do in Davis, so the four bars in town are the big hit on Thursday, Friday, and Saturday nights**. They are nothing special if you have been to clubs and bars from big cities, but they are the most entertaining places to be in Davis."

The College Prowler Take On...
Nightlife

For those under twenty-one, the nightlife experience at Davis primarily consists of frat and house parties. While sufficient for the first few years, that scene tends to get old by the time students are living off campus and old enough to drink. Unfortunately, Davis hardly offers a kicking bar scene, and it's not exactly considered a hot spot for clubs or dance halls either. Though not overly stifled by Davis' small suburban atmosphere, students seem to consider Davis' night scene left with much to be desired. They are less than impressed with the bars, and with only one club in town, it's not surprising that many get antsy. Still, considering Davis' small size, the clubs and bars are decent. To keep things fresh and entertaining, many have theme nights that manage to keep the atmosphere not so stagnant.

Luckily, Davis' neighbor city Sacramento offers many convenient options for students looking for more action. With clubs like the Rage and 815 Street, most students are easily satisfied by Sacramento's variety. For those students who are hard to please or just truly desperate, San Francisco is also another entertaining option.

The College Prowler™ Grade on

Nightlife: C+

A high grade in Nightlife indicates that there are many bars and clubs in the area that are easily accessible and affordable. Other determining factors include the number of options for the under-21 crowd and the prevalence of house parties.

Greek Life

The Lowdown On...
Greek Life

Number of Fraternities:
34

Percent of Undergrad Men in Fraternities:
6%

Number of Sororities:
18

Percent of Undergrad Women in Sororities:
7%

➜

Fraternities on Campus:

Alpha Epsilon Pi
Nu Alpha Kappa
Alpha Gamma Omega
Phi Beta Sigma
Alpha Gamma Rho
Phi Delta Theta
Chi Phi
Pi Alpha Phi
Chi Rho Omicron
Pi Kappa Alpha
Delta Chi
Psi Chi Omega
Delta Kappa Epsilon
Sigma Alpha Epsilon
Delta Lambda Phi
Sigma Alpha Mu
Delta Sigma Phi
Sigma Chi
Epsilon Sigma Rho
Sigma Kappa Rho
Gamma Zeta Alpha
Sigma Mu Delta
Kappa Alpha Psi
Sigma Phi Epsilon
Kappa Sigma
Tau Kappa Epsilon
Lambda Chi Alpha
Theta Chi
Lambda Phi Epsilon
Theta Xi

Sororities on Campus:

Alpha Chi Omega
Kappa Kappa Gamma
Alpha Delta Omega
Lambda Delta Lambda
Alpha Kappa Delta Phi
Lambda Sigma Gamma
Alpha Kappa Alpha
Lambda Theta Nu
Alpha Phi
Omega Xi Phi
Chi Delta Theta
Phi Gamma Theta
Chi Omega
Pi Beta Phi
Delta Delta Delta
Sigma Alpha
Delta Gamma
Sigma Alpha Epsilon Pi
Delta Sigma Theta
Sigma Gamma Rho
Kappa Alpha Theta
Sigma Omicron Pi

Students Speak Out On...
Greek Life

"Greek life is here. I wouldn't say it dominates. We have a lot of students, and I would say only about ten percent are in the Greek system. It's not hard to find a frat party if that's what you're looking for though."

Q "We don't bother them, and they don't bother us."

Q "The frats and sororities on campus are vocal and can be important at times, but they do not control the school at all. I would say that **being a member of a Greek Society can be very helpful socially, but at the same time you won't need it to have a good social life.**"

Q "[The Greek scene is] pretty dominant, yes. The only parties that freshmen can get into usually are rush parties—so **Greek life is big as a freshman.**"

Q "Rush week sucks. You have all these little freshmen running around with bricks in their backpacks trying to play it off like they're not getting hazed, and they run around chanting these stupid songs, pledging allegiance to their frat. **The sororities are annoying too, they have to wear these insane outfits and they all scream and giggle when they get sung to by the frats,** it's all really annoying and it seems pretty pointless."

Q "I don't think it's that bad . . . and **most frat guys aren't too molded into the stereotype.**"

Q **"I would say Greek life is pretty dominant of the social scene.** I am in a sorority, and I always have something to do on the weekends and during the week. It is a lot of fun being in the Greek system. If you choose not to join a sorority or frat, that is fine too. There are still parties on the weekends for everyone. If you are in the Greek system, you just have more parties with other members in the system during the week and on the weekends."

Q "The frat parties are usually pretty good, but the cops tend to break those up pretty quickly. **Delta Sig and AEPi always show you a good time though!"**

Q **"Greek life definitely does not dominate the social scene**, but it plays a huge part. There's at least one frat party going on each night of the weekend."

Q "The Greek life here isn't overwhelming . . . students who are in the Greek system usually have more to do on the weekends than those who aren't Greek, but they also seem a little disconnected from the rest of the campus. **Greek students pretty much interact primarily with other Greek students**, and I imagine that gets pretty old. I know the frat parties do."

Q "I'm sure there are some advantages of being Greek, I just don't see any. **Why be in the system and pay for it when you can just show up at the parties for free?** It's beyond me."

Q "The Greek life is big, and everyone has their own opinions. I think that it does dominate a little bit, but that's not a bad thing. There are parties all the time and some are invite-only. But **there are parties that anyone can go to, and they are fun, if you're into drinking and dancing."**

Q "The Greek life doesn't dominate the social scene, but it does help. I am not in a sorority, or a co-ed fraternity, nor a little sis at a frat, but I know a lot of members, and a lot of them are very funny and fun to hang out with. **You don't have to be a Greek to have fun, and you won't be pressured into it**; but if you are curious, they are very friendly, so check it out."

The College Prowler Take On...
Greek Life

About nine percent of Davis students are Greek, so it's not an overwhelming population. Frat parties do make up a significant percentage of the party scene, but students don't have to be Greek to go. For the most part, the fraternities and sororities coexist with everyone else on campus, although some students report that the Greek students rarely venture out of the system.

While most students don't mind the Greek life on campus, some reported that rush week can get a little annoying with the new pledges chanting all day long, the sorority girls singing or getting sung to, and everyone running around in togas and scrubs. However, rather than get annoyed by them, most students prefer to just laugh. Because really, when you see a big group of hot guys walking down the street and they're all wearing lipstick, what else can you do?

The College Prowler™ Grade on
Greek Life: C+

A high grade in Greek Life indicates that sororities and fraternities are not only present, but also active on campus. Other determining factors include the variety of houses available and the respect the Greek community receives from the rest of the campus.

Drug Scene

The Lowdown On...
Drug Scene

Most Prevalent Drugs on Campus:

Coffee

Alcohol

Marijuana

Tobacco

Liquor-Related Referrals:

241

Liquor-Related Arrests:

23

Drug-Related Referrals:

37

Drug-Related Arrests:

9

Drug Counseling Programs

Campus Alcohol and Other Drug Abuse Prevention Program (CADAPP)

Students Speak Out On...
Drug Scene

"Of course, drugs are present around every campus. But it's not much of an issue. Seriously, we're a bunch of nerds; we're too smart to be messing with that stuff."

Q **"I have no idea what you are talking about."**

Q "It all depends on who you make as friends. Of course, drugs are popular on college campuses, but depending on your crowd, **you can either see a lot of it or see none of it."**

Q "Drug scene? **What drug scene**?"

Q "I don't know too much about the drug scene on campus, and off campus, it's probably going on. **I know that getting caught with drugs on campus is not a fun thing to do**, and I think they will prosecute you harshly."

Q **"It's not a noticeable thing**, but there are definitely drugs circulating campus."

Q "It mostly depends on the crowd you hang out with. **People will not try to make you do drugs**. But it is present in some of the dorms. Tercero dorms are probably the most drug-free. But Cuatro is the party area and a haven for drugs."

Q "I don't see too many drugs going on. **There's quite a bit of weed, but as far as hard drugs, no, not very much."**

Q "I don't think there really is much of a drug scene. I mean, if you really wanted to get some, I'm sure you could search and find it. There are people from Humboldt and Chico going to school here, and those two areas are 'pot city,' but **you won't have to worry about crazed drug dealers shaking someone down on your way to class or something."**

Q "Wait...you mean there are drugs in Davis?"

Q "I've never seen any drugs on campus. **We have a zero-tolerance policy for drugs on campus.** [It's the] same with alcohol."

Davis students are far from overwhelmed by the drug scene. With zero-tolerance policies for drugs and alcohol on campus, students find it easy to avoid exposure to the underground network of alcohol and illegal substances. Considering the enormity of the student body, Davis' drug "problem" can practically be considered non-existent.

Not counting coffee or alcohol, the most popular Davis drug is definitely marijuana. Cigarettes are also a common sight, but weed seems to be slightly more popular. That said, it's a very subjective situation: drugs (both legal and illegal) are easy to get and easy to stay from. It's just a matter of meeting and getting to know like-minded people.

The College Prowler™ Grade on
Drug Scene: A-

A high grade in the Drug Scene indicates that drugs are not a noticeable part of campus life; drug use is not visible, and no pressure to use them seems to exist.

Campus Strictness

The Lowdown On...
Campus Strictness

What Are You Most Likely to Get Caught Doing on Campus?

- Having an open container of alcohol
- Downloading copyrighted material
- Loud music in the dorms
- Biking under the influence

Students Speak Out On...
Campus Strictness

"The campus police are generally not overly strict on drinking although with drugs the campus police is the least of your worries . . . the student council for academic affairs is very strict."

Q "No idea; never got caught."

Q "The cops here have nothing to do, so **they just have too much time on their hands and jump at you for anything**. I got pulled over on my bike for not stopping at a stop sign (how many bikers stop at stop signs?!) and he [wasn't nice] about it. He could tell I was a little irritated, so he gave me another ticket for not having the right reflectors on my back wheel. It was so lame."

Q **"They are extremely strict.** Let me just say you've heard of a DUI, well here we give out what's called a BUI—biking under the influence. Just don't do it on campus."

Q **"The campus police are not very invasive**, just keep it under wraps."

Q "We never had any problems. The cops broke up a few parties we were at, but nobody got in trouble. Most are nice after finals because they know we've been under lots of stress and have been practically living at the library for the last few days, so they don't care that we get a little crazy after the last tests. Sometimes though, **they can be jerks if they think you're disrupting other students who may be studying."**

Q "**Campus police are pretty strict on drugs and drinking on campus.** There are always cops around the town and the apartments. There are also cops on bikes that can give biking tickets out for people under the influence."

Q "The police are pretty bad with the drinking; they'll get you. **The open container law is really lame, and that's their favorite thing to bust you for.**"

Q "Not very strict at all. **Depending on which dorm you are in, you can get away with a lot of stuff.** Lots of people smoke on campus. Not much drinking except at parties."

Q "**The police officers are really strict.** They're kind of jerks. They really like to pick on the college students—so you really have to watch out."

The College Prowler Take On...
Campus Strictness

Many students have never had to deal with campus authorities. In the dorms, if students are caught with either alcohol or drugs, they receive a written referral to a Student Judicial Board, and the board decides what sort of consequences to implement. So while it's nice that your fate is in the hands of your understanding peers, there are some things that are not tolerated. Drinking and driving is not something where students are likely to "get off easy," and even if you ride your bike while you're drunk, you may end up with a BUI (Biking under the influence) and have your driver's license pulled. Davis considers a bike to be a vehicle, and there are severe consequences for being irresponsible and operating vehicles.

Generally, students consider the campus to be exasperatingly strict. Between BUIs, parking tickets, and fines for not having a bike light at night, students claim that security is unnecessarily strict, and that campus police enjoy ticketing young college students. However, most had no problems abiding by the regulations (or keeping offences under wraps), and the low campus crime rate is undoubtedly due in part to the tight campus security.

The College Prowler™ Grade on
Campus Strictness: C

A high Campus Strictness grade implies an overall lenient atmosphere; police and RAs are fairly tolerant, and the administration's rules are flexible.

Parking

The Lowdown On...
Parking

Approximate Parking Permit Cost
$200-$500

UCD Parking Services:
Transportation and Parking Services: (530) 752-8277
www.taps.ucdavis.edu/parking

Student Parking Lot?
Yes

Freshman Allowed to Park?
No

Common Parking Tickets:
Expired Meter: $22
No Permit: $30

Parking Permits

Permits are not issued to freshmen, but students who work downtown can apply for city permits. Chances are slim, but that's the option with the highest chance of success.

Did You Know?

Best Places to Find a Parking Spot
MU parking structure

Good Luck Getting a Parking Spot Here!
On the streets by the dorms

Students Speak Out On...
Parking

> **"Parking is generally not that bad as long as you have a parking permit."**

Q "If you don't live on campus, you get a C permit, and it's possible to park, theoretically, but sometimes you spend a lot of time driving around the myriad of lots looking for a space. ASUCD runs the bus system around town (free for undergrads) and they can get you anywhere, so you don't need to drive to school. **If you live on campus, it's easier with a resident permit in the resident lots."**

Q "You are better off bringing a bike to get around campus, or buy one here. Just a bit of trivia: **Davis has the highest bike-per-capita ratio than any other city in the entire world** except for Amsterdam. Interesting, no?"

Q "I don't have a car but I've heard horror stories. **Stick with public trans or use your bike or skateboard."**

Q **"Compared to UCLA or other schools, parking is pretty good.** The only time parking gets really hard to find on campus is during the winter. During those months, they usually bring in parking attendants and they stack park your car. It is still kind of hard to find parking so your best bet is to take the bus. You usually have to walk farther from the parking lots than you do from the bus stops anyway."

Q "It is definitely not easy to park. **Freshmen are not allowed cars, so it can be very difficult to park on the streets** for freshmen. For upper classmen, I hear it is also very hard to park on campus, even if you have a parking permit."

Q **"Parking sucks!** It's easier to pogo-stick your way to class!"

Q **"The parking is awful** . . . there's a reason bikes are so popular."

Q "Parking is horrible, especially for freshman because they don't give you parking permits. **If you drive on campus for class, plan to leave a little earlier than you thought."**

Q "Because the school is growing so fast, the parking is crazy. **I would recommend leaving your car at one place and travel via bike, walk, bus, car pool, etc.** The bus system is so awesome that most people don't usually drive, unless they are commuting from outside of Davis."

The College Prowler Take On...
Parking

Students unabashedly admit that parking on campus is miserable. Actually, parking anywhere in Davis is seen as pretty awful. They don't ride bikes without reason! The parking situation was so bad that starting fall quarter of 2002, freshmen weren't allowed to bring cars. The school refuses to issue freshmen parking permits (unless they have an absolutely valid reason), but it doesn't seem to phase most of the student body. Most prefer to just get around on bikes or the bus, and the public transportation at Davis more than compensates for the impossible parking.

On campus, students tend to think that a car is really just a pain. One of the parking lots on campus was paid for entirely by parking tickets: that says something. However, cars provide many much needed opportunities to venture outside of Davis, not only for the San Francisco parties, but many internships at the Med Center are in Sacramento, and cars are a luxury to have. Though the Davis parking is terrible, it's not a big deal if you're on a bike, and most people are on bikes anyway. So it's not as awful as it sounds.

The College Prowler™ Grade on

Parking: C-

A high grade in this section indicates that parking is both available and affordable, and that parking enforcement isn't overly severe.

Transportation

The Lowdown On...
Transportation

Ways to Get Around Town:
Bike

Unitrans

University Shuttles

Walking

On Campus:
Bike

Walk

Public Transportation:
Unitrans

Yolobus

Car Rentals

Car Rentals
Alamo,
national: (800) 327-9633
www.alamo.com

Avis, national: (800) 831-2847,
www.avis.com

Budget,
national: (800) 527-0700,
www.budget.com

Dollar,
national: (800) 800-4000.
www.dollar.com

Enterprise,
national: (800) 736-8222,
www.enterprise.com

Hertz, national: (800) 654-3131,
www.hertz.com

National,
national: (800) 227-7368,
www.nationalcar.com

Best Way to Get Around Town:

Bike, hands down. If it's raining, the bus is a good option.

Ways to Get Out of Town

Airlines Serving Sacramento:

American Airlines, (800) 433-7300, www.americanairlines.com

Continental, (800) 523-3273, www.continental.com

Delta, (800) 221-1212, www.delta-air.com

Northwest, (800) 225-2525, www.nwa.com

Southwest, (800) 435-9792, www.southwest.com

TWA, (800) 221-2000, www.twa.com

United, (800) 241-6522, www.united.com

US Airways, (800) 428-4322, www.usairways.com

Airport:

Sacramento International

How to Get There:

Davis Airporter

A Shuttle ride to the Airport Costs: $25

Greyhound

www.greyhound.com
(800)231-2222

Amtrak

The Amtrak Station is downtown, approximately one mile from campus.

http://www.amtrakwest.com
(800) 872-7245

Students Speak Out On...
Transportation

"The public transportation is very good. All students get free public transportation. It's the [university's] way of trying to mitigate the parking issues on campus."

"Very convenient, and **don't forget Tipsy Taxi!"**

"Everything for the most part is in walking distance from the campus and dorms, whether or not you want to walk (or bike) is a different story, but the bus system is pretty good. There are buses going everywhere in Davis—to the campus or downtown."

"Public Transportation at Davis is very convenient. Most people do ride their bikes, but if for some reason you don't feel like it, **Unitrans is a wonderful system.** I found myself only riding the bus towards the end of the year, because it is just a lot easier and takes less effort."

"Davis is probably one of the easy towns to get around as a student. The area is very flat so you can easily bike or walk from place to place. If cardiovascular fitness is not your style, the university has buses running all over town constantly making it easy to get from place to place."

"The Amtrak station is not far from campus and is located in downtown Davis. **Sacramento International Airport is only about twenty minutes away.** The Yolo bus makes stops all over Davis town and campus, and it goes to the airport."

Q "You can't really leave Davis unless you take the county buses. However, **the ASUCD bus system is great and gets you around all parts of town.** Still, having a car is preferable. The buses are more designed to take you to and from school. Taking a bus to get to the market wouldn't work so well."

Q **"The public transportation outweighs the hassle of bringing a car."**

Q "Public transportation is scheduled very well all across town. **Students don't even pay for the bus."**

The College Prowler Take On...
Transportation

Students have overwhelmingly positive remarks about the public transportation, and their favorite part is the price—with a student ID, the bus system is absolutely free. Students seem to appreciate the university's attempt to lessen the effects of the parking crisis on campus, and feel that the public transportation compensates nicely for the packed parking lots.

Besides being such a bargain, public transportation is surprisingly efficient. The bus system covers most of Davis, and students don't usually have to wait long before a bus comes. It may be a good idea to catch an earlier bus than you need, because sometimes they can be off-schedule; depending on traffic, the buses can be anywhere from ten minutes ahead or ten minutes behind. Generally, the further away from campus you are, the less punctual the bus. But for being run by students, Unitrans is really impressive—and a lifesaver when your bike has a flat and it is pouring rain.

The College Prowler™ Grade on

Transportation: A-

A high grade for Transportation indicates that campus buses, public buses, cabs, and rental cars are readily-available and affordable. Other determining factors include proximity to an airport and the necessity of transportation.

Weather

The Lowdown On...
Weather

Average Temperature

Fall: 65°F
Winter: 51 °F
Spring: 74 °F
Summer: 93 °F

Average Precipitation

Fall: 3.16 in.
Winter: 9.94 in.
Spring: 4.02 in.
Summer: 0.19 in.

Students Speak Out On...
Weather

"Well, it's typical California weather . . some mild seasons, but some extreme summers and winters. If you have allergies, bring plenty of Allegra for the spring unless you want to sit in your room all day and miss the gorgeous weather!"

Q "Cold in the winter, hot in the summer. Wait—**HOT, HOT, HOT in the Summer!"**

Q **"Well the winters are cold, and the summers are hot!** So as long as [the clothing] covers your body you'll get at least some use out of it."

Q "I personally love the weather . . . some people complain that it gets too hot in August, but I love it. The only thing I'd caution you about is the pollen and stuff in the air. **Davis . . . can wreak havoc on those allergies."**

Q "The weather goes from one extreme to the next. Bring very warm winter clothes to light summer clothes and everything in between, also—**be prepared for rain!"**

Q **"Davis weather is not that great, but it depends where you are coming from.** I come from Los Angeles, so Northern California weather is completely opposite [of] nice Southern California weather. It is pretty cold in the winter, and it rains a lot in the spring. The summers get very hot though. I would bring all kinds of clothes; jackets for the winter and summer clothes for the summertime."

Q **"Davis has four very distinct seasons, and you'll need clothing for all of them.** Definitely bring some waterproof clothes for those bike rides in the pouring November rain—parkas are a must. The poor unfortunate souls who leave their snowboarding jackets at home are destined to ride the streets wearing garbage bags . . . trust me, it's not fun. Also, be sure to bring a pair of good gloves: hands are the first things to go numb when you're on a bike. You'll also need some light clothes for June when it's 110 outside . . . some shorts and tank tops are a good idea. But ladies, keep in mind: you'll be on a bike, do you really think miniskirts are a good idea? Don't forget a swimsuit for the Rec Pool and some clothes to work out in, just in case you decide to join an IM team or take advantage of the free gym access. You also may want to bring something nice to wear to the Mondavi Center (it's a pretty formal theatre), a robe if you're in a communal bathroom, and clothes that you can trash if a rainy day calls for a game of mud football. And of course, what no Davis student can do without—a UCD sweatshirt."

Q **"Winters are freezing and summers are boiling— expect extremes**, but the fall and spring seasons are beautiful."

The College Prowler Take On...
Weather

Regarding the Davis weather, students replied with very consistent responses and concluded that Davis weather is extreme. From the sizzling August heat to the numbing November rain, Davis weather covers a whole spectrum of atmospheric activity, even getting snow every few years. Students are advised to prepare for extreme seasons and bring a wardrobe packed with everything from snow gear to bathing suits. For those with allergies, medication is also a good idea—with all the construction and agriculture, allergies tend to flare up in the spring.

Despite Davis' tendency to have extreme summers and winters, it gets its share of the unbeatable California weather. Overall, the climate is comfortable, and in a town where the sun shines an average of 288 days a year, even Southern California students shouldn't have to worry about being depressed by the weather.

B-

The College Prowler™ Grade on

Weather: B-

A high Weather grade designates that temperatures are mild and rarely reach extremes, that the campus tends to be sunny rather than rainy, and that weather is fairly consistent rather than unpredictable.

Report Card Summary

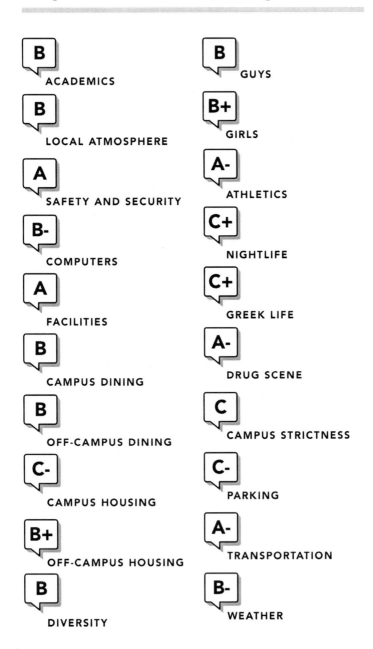

B ACADEMICS

B LOCAL ATMOSPHERE

A SAFETY AND SECURITY

B- COMPUTERS

A FACILITIES

B CAMPUS DINING

B OFF-CAMPUS DINING

C- CAMPUS HOUSING

B+ OFF-CAMPUS HOUSING

B DIVERSITY

B GUYS

B+ GIRLS

A- ATHLETICS

C+ NIGHTLIFE

C+ GREEK LIFE

A- DRUG SCENE

C CAMPUS STRICTNESS

C- PARKING

A- TRANSPORTATION

B- WEATHER

Overall Experience

Students Speak Out On...
Overall Experience

"I am really glad I came to Davis. I met a bunch of wonderful people, I love the town and the campus is beautiful. The atmosphere is very nice; especially when the weather warms up...everyone seems to be happy and relaxed."

"Regrets? Are you kidding me? **Davis is the best thing that has ever happened to me.** I've met some of the coolest people in my life here, and for once, I actually love [school.] Not tolerating it, but loving it. Strange, but true . . . and plus, if I hadn't gone here, I never would have met my girlfriend."

Q "**My college experience here so far has been great.** I am glad I made the decision to come here instead of Berkeley or UCLA. The atmosphere is so chill and laid-back; I cannot ask for more. I love UC Davis. I wouldn't go anywhere else."

Q "I really like it here. I have no regrets about Davis. **It's the best environment for my major [and] my liberal attitude,** and I feel like there are opportunities to explore any avenue of academics, social life, and activities in general."

Q "Overall, I loved Davis. It took some getting used to, but it was a great experience. **You have to meet the right people, because it is a really small town.** You have to be willing to put up with the small town life. If I had to do it all over again, there would be no hesitation: I would definitely go to Davis all over again. It was the best time of my life, and I loved it. The only thing you need to keep in mind is the small town factor. If you like big towns and nice clubs and bars, then Davis is not the place for you. If you are laid back and like the laziness of a small town, then you will love Davis."

Q "I absolutely love Davis and the people I have met there. I cannot picture myself anywhere but Davis. **It is a great place to learn, socialize, and just have a great time!**"

Q The **school is great; it's all what you make of it.** You have to get involved, go out, and explore or Davis can be a really boring place."

Q "I love Davis. **I love the small town atmosphere.** I love that we have cows on campus. I love being able to ride my bike for five minutes and find myself in the middle of some farm road, in the middle of nowhere. I love being able to drive my car ten minutes and end up at a varied social scene in Sacramento. I love being so close to the Sierra Nevada to ski and hike. The only thing I miss is the ocean."

Q "I think it's great here. **I like biking around and not feeling like I need a car.** The campus is good-looking and there are tons of trees everywhere. We are close to snowboarding (at Lake Tahoe) and the people are really nice. I've met some of the coolest people ever here and I wouldn't change it for anything. I also like that it is a college town. It has the benefits of a major school, without any hassles."

Q **"Aggies all the way Baby! No regrets!"**

Q "I could not be happier with my decision to attend UC Davis. **Everyday I am surrounded by brilliant, talented people, people so diverse but with commonalities too.** I love everything about Davis: the trees, the community, even the cows. I love the fact that I came in planning to major in Biochemistry, changed to Psychology, then to English, and still may end up going to med school. I have learned so much and feel so privileged to be part of this amazing group of people, I could not be happier anywhere else on earth, and have no regrets about choosing to be an Aggie."

Q **"Davis wasn't my first choice school, but I've actually enjoyed my first year here.** I do, however, wish I were at a school near the beach. But then again, I might never go to class so I'm glad I'm here at Davis."

Q "I love it here in Davis. **There [are] always people to meet, things to do, and classes to skip."**

The College Prowler Take On...
Overall Experience

Overall, students seem to really enjoy their time at the University of California at Davis. At UCD, students are granted unprecedented opportunities to excel academically, alongside expert professors who exhibit genuine interest in sharing their knowledge. With such a friendly campus and such competitive academics, many enjoy the dynamics between the bustling, active university and the laid-back college town. Some even get a little fond of the cows after a while!

Despite the frustratingly intense course load, fizzling nightlife, and blazing summers, UC Davis usually leaves its students feeling glad that they came. Studying at Davis is a unique experience, and the education you leave with remains with you for the rest of your life. Not only are you likely to leave Davis with a priceless diploma and a starting salary that makes up for all those weekends spent in Shields, but you'll also leave with friends, memories, and the experience of a lifetime. Sure, there are some things here that are somewhat different: Davis is a big school in a small town; there are cows on campus, and bikes. And there are protests for practically every decision Congress decides to make. It's active. For prospective students who crave diversity and challenge, it may just be perfect.

The Inside Scoop

The Lowdown On...
The Inside Scoop

UCD Slang

Know the slang, know the school. The following is a list of things you really need to know before coming to UCD. The more of these words you know, the better off you'll be.

Bike Barn- A barn near the Silo where students can get their bikes serviced.

The Cow Dorms- Tercero dorms

The CoHo- The Coffeehouse, an on-campus restaurant.

DC- Dining Commons

The Deathstar- The Social Science Building

First Pass- A student's first chance to register for classes online.

Funny Farm- Primate Center

L&S- Letters and Science, Less Stress, Lazy and Sexy

LRC- Learning Resourse Center

The MU- The Memorial Union, the main student center on campus.

The Quad- A grassy area between the MU and Shield's Library.

RA- Resident Advisor

Sac/Sactown- Sacramento

Second Pass- A student's second chance to register, usually several weeks after the first pass.

"UCD'd out"- wearing UC Davis apparell

Veg/Veggie- vegan/vegetarian

WebEm- A nickname for Webster and Emerson dorm buildings.

Things I Wish I Knew Before Coming to UC Davis

- How to change a bike tire.
- How to manage time better.
- How to read bus schedules.
- Get on the smallest meal plan possible.
- It's not a huge party school.
- How hard the course load is.
- How to study with lots of background noise.
- How many options there are.
- Study for the diagnostic tests to avoid wasting an entire quarter.
- Don't be afraid to change your major.

Tips to Succeed at UC Davis

- Take a light load your first quarter.
- Don't ever fall behind.
- Go to discussions even if they are optional.
- Take classes that interest you.
- Actually go to class.
- Go to office hours.
- Use the library as often as possible.
- Ask questions.
- Get some fresh air after studying all day.
- Put off declaring a major for as long as possible.

School Spirit

Davis has such inspiring school spirit! Besides packing the stadium for football games, hanging out on Picnic Day, and plastering the UC Davis logo over much of their clothing, Davis students show their school pride in the support they show for each other. Plays on campus are often sold out, wild and screaming fans attend nearly every sporting event, and student clubs thrive off of the initiative of the student body; there is an abundance of school spirit. Students here will cheer on just about anything, unless of course, they decide to protest it.

Incidentally, Davis students are known for their spirited picket lines, boycotts, and sit-ins. Campus bulletin boards are feathered with flyers advertising different protests—everything from the increased student fees to Proctor and Gamble's animal testing to the mobilization of troops. Generally, UCD students are very informed about issues they feel strongly about, and they don't hesitate to share their views. Students are loud and proud, and, though there are occasional discrepancies between students, all perspectives are usually heard and respected.

Traditions

Picnic Day

This is the college version of the high school Open House. Picnic Day takes place in early April and showcases the work of many departments. There are pig races, petting zoos, a car show with the College of Engineering's electric cars, booths for student organizations, food, music, etc. Picnic Day is a popular day for students, alumni, and prospective students to come get a feel for UCD.

Finding a Job or Internship

The Lowdown On...
Finding a Job or Internship

Davis has the largest Internship and Career Center in the nation- just stop by the office on campus or visit the website to get a code for your internship search.

icc.ucdavis.edu

Advice:

Start looking for internships early, before the quarter you want them. Many positions require applications, and some can be competitive. Most require multi-quarter commitments, so be sure you're applying for something you can stick with for several weeks. The earlier you start your internship search, the better your chances of landing a good position!

Career Center Resources & Services:

Internship and Career Center

South Hall

icc.ucdavis.edu

Average Salary Information
The Lowdown:

Within one year following graduation, 64% of Davis students report working full time. Twenty-six percent of these graduates obtained jobs before leaving UC Davis; 92% were working full time within 6 months of graduation. Their average salary was $38,700, with engineers and computer/math/physical scientists reporting the highest salaries ($52,500, $49,700, respectively). Nearly 4/5 obtained jobs in their chosen fields, and most surveyed said they were "very well" or "more than adequately" prepared at UC Davis for their initial employment.

% of Grads who enter job market within 2 years after graduation:

84%

Alumni

The Lowdown On...
Alumni

About Alumni
Cal Aggie Alumni Association

Website:
www.alumni.ucdavis.edu

Office:
Cal Aggie Alumni Association
One Shields Avenue
University of California
Davis, Ca
95616-8517
(530) 752-0286
(800) 242-4723
alumni@ucdavis.edu

Services Available:
Free e-mail
Newsletter
Career resources
Discounts on products and services
Library access
Recreation access
Discounts at sporting events

Major Alumni Events

CAAA Alumni Awards

Picnic Day

UC Day Legislative Conference

UC Davis Homecoming

Alumni Publications

CAAA Alumni Awards

Picnic Day

UC Day Legislative Conference

UC Davis Homecoming

Did You Know?

Famous UCD Alumni:

Gus Lee, attorney and author; China Boy Martin Yan, chef and host of Yan Can Cook; Mark and Delia Owens, zoologists, ecologists, and authors of, Cry of the Kalahari and The Eye of the Elephant; Ken O'Brien, former quarterback for the New York Jets

Student Organizations

Student Organizations

Minority Student Organizations:
African-American Health Sciences Association

Asian Law Students Association

Asian Student Union

Black Law Students Association

Chicano/Latino Medical Students Association

Chinese American Student Association

Cross-Culture Coalition

Filipino Americans in Medicine

Hmong Student Union

LaRaza Student Association

Masala

Mga Kapatid

Mujeres Ayudando LaRaza

NaKeikio Hawaii Nei

Native American Law Student Association

Pan-African Student Association

United Filipino-American Student Association

Campus-based Religious Organizations:

Bahai Club

Bible Christian Fellowship Gospel Choir

Cal Aggie Christian Association

Campus Advance for Christ

Canterbury Episcopal Club

Chi Alpha Christian Fellowship

Christian Science Organization

Christian Student Union

Christian Vietnamese Fellowship

Christians on Campus

College English Fellowship

College Life

Intervarsity Christian Fellowship

Jewish Student Union

Latter-Day Saints Student Association

Lutheran Student Movement

Mahayana

Muslim Student Association

Newman Student Catholic Community

International Student Organizations:

American Field Service

Davis Anime Club

Chinese Student and Scholar Fellowship

Filipino Association for Health Careers

Hong Kong Student Union

International Association of Business Communicators International Law Society

International Vet Student Association

Japanese Student Union

Korean Student Association

Taiwan Chinese Student Society

Vietnamese Student Association

Other Student Organizations:

Square dance

Modern dance and Ballroom dance groups

Comedy Troupe

Model United Nations

AIDS Education Project

Astronomy Club

Block and Bridle

Coalition Against Genocide

Parents Under Pressure

Wildlife Society

Visually Impaired Persons

The Best & The Worst

The Ten BEST Things About UC Davis:

1	The people
2	The campus
3	Downtown
4	The school spirit Picnic Day and the Whole Earth Festival
5	The educational opportunities
6	Diversity
7	The Mondavi Center
8	The T-1 connection in the dorms
9	Farmers Market
10	The Internship and Career Center

The Ten **WORST** Things About UC Davis:

1 No Parking!

2 Dealing with Administration

3 Off-campus housing prices

4 Late charges on registration fees

5 Open Container law

6 Instructors with thick accents

7 No convenience stores

8 7:30 a.m. lectures

9 Lack of entertainment

10 Cows

Visiting
UC Davis

The Lowdown On...
Visiting UCD

Hotel Information

Aggie Inn-
245 First Street,
Davis (530) 756-0352

Davis Bed and Breakfast Inn-
422 A Street,
Davis (530) 753-9611

Econo Lodge-
221 D Street,
Davis (530) 756-1040

Hallmark Inn-
110 F Street,
Davis (530) 753-3600

Palm Court Hotel-
234 D Street,
Davis (530) 753-7100

University Inn-
340 A Street,
Davis (530) 756-8648

University Lodge-
123 B Street,
Davis (530) 756-7890

Take a Campus Virtual Tour

www.ucdavis.edu/about.html

Campus Tours

Guided campus tours are offered in the spring, but feel free to visit anytime! Picnic Day is often the most popular day to visit.

Weekday general walking tours can be scheduled one week in advance by phoning (530) 752-8111 or visiting our online registration website. Weekday walking tours are normally conducted at 10 a.m. and 2 p.m. If a one-week advanced notice is not possible, you may be able to add your party to an existing tour, if one has been scheduled. The tour is 90 minutes long, student-lead, and consists of a walk through the main center core of the UC Davis campus. We cover approximately 600 acres of the 5,200 acre campus. When phoning our campus tours office, we will be happy to speak with you about any questions you may have regarding UC Davis. After scheduling your tour, we will mail you a confirmation letter, accompanied by a map and directions on how to drive to our campus.

Advising from Admissions is available on a drop-in basis Monday through Friday from the hours of 9 a.m. to 12 p.m. and 1 p.m. to 4 p.m., except on observed holidays.

We recommend casual attire and comfortable walking shoes.

The weather in Davis is very mild and beautiful during most of the spring and fall. During the winter, Davis receives, on average, 17.5 inches of rain, and the temperature rarely reaches freezing. Summers in Davis are very dry, and temperatures can climb into the high 90s and low 100s.

For more information call (530) 752-8111.

Directions to Campus

From the San Francisco Bay Area:

Take Interstate 80 East toward Sacramento.

Exit at UC Davis.

From Sacramento:

Take Interstate 80 West toward San Francisco.

Exit at UC Davis.

From Sacramento International Airport:

Take Interstate 5 South toward Sacramento and follow the signs to Interstate 80 West toward San Francisco.

Exit at UC Davis.

From Woodland:

Take Highway 113 South to Interstate 80, then east toward Sacramento.

Exit at UC Davis.

From Los Angeles:

Take Interstate 5 North toward Sacramento and follow the signs to Interstate 80 West toward San Francisco.

Exit at UC Davis.

From the UC Davis exit:

Exit off Interstate 80, take Old Davis Road to the campus core area. Pass the South Gate Information Kiosk (or stop for further information). Continue onto the loop road, which circles the campus core area. Visitor parking lots are marked. Purchase a $5 all-day parking permit on weekdays from the bright yellow permit dispenser. Permit dispensers will accept quarters, one-dollar bills, Visa or MasterCard. Parking on weekends is free, except during special events.

Words to Know

Academic Probation – A student can receive this if they fail to keep up with their school's academic minimums. Those who are unable to improve their grades after receiving this warning can possibly face dismissal.

Beer Pong / Beirut – A drinking game with numerous cups of beer arranged in a particular pattern on each side of a table. The goal is to get a ping pong ball into one of the opponent's cups by throwing the ball or hitting it with a paddle. If the ball lands in a cup, the opponent is required to drink the beer.

Bid – An invitation from a fraternity or sorority to pledge their specific house.

Blue-Light Phone – Brightly-colored phone posts with a blue light bulb on top. These phones exist for security purposes and are located at various outside locations around most campuses. If a student has an emergency or is feeling endangered, they can pick up one of these phones (free of charge) to connect with campus police or an escort service.

Campus Police – Policemen who are specifically assigned to a given institution. Campus police are not regular city officers; they are employed by the university in a full-time capacity.

Club Sports – A level of sports that falls somewhere between varsity and intramural. If a student is unable to commit to a varsity team but has a lot of passion for athletics, a club sport could be a better, less intense option. If a club sport still requires too much commitment, intramurals often involve no traveling and a lot less time.

Cocaine – An illegal drug. Also known as "coke" or "blow," cocaine often resembles a white crystalline or powdery substance. It is highly addictive and dangerous.

Common Application – An application that students can use to apply to multiple schools.

Course Registration – The time when a student selects what courses they would like for the upcoming quarter or semester. Prior to registration, it is best to have an idea of several back-up courses in case a particular class becomes full. If a course is full, a student can place themselves on the waitlist, although this still does not guarantee entry.

Division Athletics – Athletics range from Division I to Division III. Division IA is the most competitive, while Division III is considered to be the least competitive.

Dorm – Short for dormitory, a dorm is an on-campus housing facility. Dorms can provide a range of options from suite-style rooms to more communal options that include shared bathrooms. Most first-year students live in dorms. Some upperclassmen who wish to stay on campus also choose this option.

Early Action – A way to apply to a school and get an early acceptance response without a binding commitment. This is a system that is becoming less and less available.

Early Decision – An option that students should use only if they are positive that a place is their dream school. If a student applies to a school using the early decision option and is admitted, they are required and bound to attend that university. Admission rates are usually higher with early decision students because the school knows that a student is making them their first choice.

Ecstasy – An illegal drug. Also known as "E" or "X," ecstasy looks like a pill and most resembles an aspirin. Considered a party drug, ecstasy is very dangerous and can be deadly.

Ethernet – An extremely fast internet connection that is usually available in most university-owned residence halls. To use an Ethernet connection properly, a student will need a network card and cable for their computer.

Fake ID – A counterfeit identification card that contains false information. Most commonly, students get fake IDs and change their birthdates so that they appear to be older than 21 (of legal drinking age). Even though it is illegal, many college students have fake IDs in hopes of purchasing alcohol or getting into bars.

Frosh – Slang for "freshmen."

Hazing – Initiation rituals that must be completed for membership into some fraternities or sororities. Numerous universities have outlawed hazing due to its degrading or dangerous requirements.

Sports (IMs) – A popular, and usually free, student activity where students create teams and compete against other groups for fun. These sports vary in competitiveness and can include a range of activities—everything from billiards to water polo. IM sports are a great way to meet people with similar interests.

Keg – Officially called a half barrel, a keg contains roughly 200 12-ounce servings of beer and is often found at college parties.

LSD – An illegal drug. Also known as acid, this hallucinogenic drug most commonly resembles a tab of paper.

Marijuana – An illegal drug. Also known as weed or pot; besides alcohol, marijuana is one of the most commonly-found drugs on campuses across the country.

Major –The focal point of a student's college studies; a specific topic that is studied for a degree. Examples of majors include physics, English, history, computer science, economics, business, and music. Many students decide on a specific major before arriving on campus, while others are simply "undecided" and figure it out later. Those who are extremely interested in two areas can also choose to double major.

Meal Block – The equivalent of one meal. Students on a "meal plan" usually receive a fixed number of meals per week.

Each meal, or "block," can be redeemed at the school's dining facilities in place of cash. More often than not, if a student fails to use their weekly allotment of meal blocks, they will be forfeited.

Minor – An additional focal point in a student's education. Often serving as a compliment or addition to a student's main area of focus, a minor has fewer requirements and prerequisites to fulfill than a major. Minors are not required for graduation from most schools; however some students who want to further explore many different interests choose to have both a major and a minor.

Mushrooms – An illegal drug. Also known as "shrooms," this drug looks like regular mushrooms but are extremely hallucinogenic.

Off-Campus Housing – Housing from a particular landlord or rental group that is not affiliated with the university. Depending on the college, off-campus housing can range from extremely popular to non-existent. Those students who choose to live off campus are typically given more freedom, but they also have to deal with things such as possible subletting scenarios, furniture, and bills. In addition to these factors, rental prices and distance often affect a student's decision to move off campus.

Office Hours – Time that teachers set aside for students who have questions about the coursework. Office hours are a good place for students to go over any problems and to show interest in the subject material.

Pledging – The time after a student has gone through rush, received a bid, and has chosen a particular fraternity or sorority they would like to join. Pledging usually lasts anywhere from one to two semesters. Once the pledging period is complete and a particular student has done everything that is required to become a member, they are considered a brother or sister. If a fraternity or a sorority would decide to "haze" a group of students, these initiation rituals would take place during the pledging period.

Private Institution – A school that does not use taxpayers dollars to help subsidize education costs. Private schools typically cost more than public schools and are usually smaller.

Prof – Slang for "professor."

Public Institution – A school that uses taxpayers dollars to help subsidize education costs. Public schools are often a good value for in-state residents and tend to be larger than most private colleges.

Quarter System (sometimes referred to as the Trimester System) – A type of academic calendar system. In this setup, students take classes for three academic periods. The first quarter usually starts in late September or early October and concludes right before Christmas. The second quarter usually starts around early to mid–January and finishes up around March or April. The last quarter, or "third quarter," usually starts in late March or early April and finishes up in late May or Mid-June. The fourth quarter is summer. The major difference between the quarter system and semester system is that students take more courses but with less coverage.

RA (Resident Assistant) – A student leader who is assigned to a particular floor in a dormitory in order to help to the other students who live there. A RA's duties include ensuring student safety and providing guidance or assistance wherever possible.

Recitation – An extension of a specific course; a "review" session of sorts. Because some classes are so large, recitations offer a setting with fewer students where students can ask questions and get help from professors or TAs in a more personalized environment. As a result, it is common for most large lecture classes to be supplemented with recitations.

Rolling Admissions – A form of admissions. Most commonly found at public institutions, schools with this type of policy continue to accept students throughout the year until their class sizes are met. For example, some schools begin accepting students as early as December and will continue to do so until April or May.

Room and Board – This is typically the combined cost of a university-owned room and a meal plan.

Room Draw/Housing Lottery – A common way to pick on-campus room assignments for the following year. If a student decides to remain in university-owned housing, they are assigned a unique number that, along with seniority, is used to choose their new rooms for the next year.

Rush – The period in which students can meet the brothers and sisters of a particular chapter and find out if a given fraternity or sorority is right for them. Rushing a fraternity or a sorority is not a requirement at any school. The goal of rush is to give students who are serious about pledging a feel for what to expect.

Semester System – The most common type of academic calendar system at college campuses. This setup typically includes two semesters in a given school year. The "fall" semester starts around the end of August or early September and finishes right before winter vacation. The "spring" semester usually starts in mid-January and ends around late April or May.

Student Center/Rec Center/Student Union – A common area on campus that often contains study areas, recreation facilities, and eateries. This building is often a good place to meet up with fellow students and is most commonly used as a hangout. Depending on the school, the student center can have a huge role or a non-existent role in campus life.

Student ID – A university-issued photo ID that serves as a student's key to many different functions within an institution. Some schools require students to show these cards in order to get into dorms, libraries, cafeterias, and other facilities. In addition to storing meal plan information, in some cases, a student ID can actually work as a debit card and allow students to purchase things from bookstores or local shops.

Suite – A type of dorm room. Unlike other places that have communal bathrooms that are shared by the entire floor, a suite has a private bathroom. Suite-style dorm rooms can house anywhere from two to ten students.

TA (Teacher's Assistant) – An undergraduate or grad student who helps in some manner with a specific course. In some cases, a TA will teach a class, assist a professor, grade assignments, or conduct office hours.

Undergraduate – A student who is in the process of studying for their Bachelor (college) degree.

ABOUT THE AUTHOR:

Writing this book has been a wonderful experience. After finally declaring myself as an English major, I decided to plunge into the field and try my hand at freelance writing. This book is the fruit of my labors. Hopefully, it is the start of a future career in creative writing, and the start of a line of publications. I have always been fascinated by language, but what little background I have has been rooted in poetry. This book was a wonderful and challenging opportunity to expand my horizon, and I hope it offers insightful information about Davis. Currently I'm a sophomore at UCD tirelessly working towards degrees in English and some branch of science that I haven't decided on yet—possibly Microbiology or Environmental Science. Continuing my education here has been a dizzying and inspiring experience; I only hope that this guidebook captured some of that unquantifiable spirit. I learned a lot in the process of writing it; I hope you get something out of it too.

I owe many people heaps of thanks for all their support during this whole experience. Thank you Mom and Dad for your faith in me, Beez for your humor, Grandma and Papa for understanding when I had to cancel plans to meet the deadlines, Aunt Deed, Uncle Keith, and the girls for the Internet connection, Adam, Donry, Laura, Gracie-Lou, Ross-Hintze's, and Adelaide for your support. Danny, Benji, Danielle, Jack, Marge, Nina, Mari-Ferrari, Matt, and everyone else who obligingly answered the surveys, and all my roomies for broadening my perspective and enriching my college experience. Thank you Mr. Clark for getting this whole show on the road, and many thanks to everyone at College Prowler! Email me at tristenchang@collegeprowler.com with any questions!

Notes

Notes

....

....

....

....

....

....

....

....

....

....

....

....

....

Notes

....

....

....

....

....

....

....

....

....

....

....

....

....

Notes

Notes

....

....

....

....

....

....

....

....

....

....

....

....

....

Notes

....

....

....

....

....

....

....

....

....

....

....

....

....

Notes

Notes

....

....

....

....

....

....

....

....

....

....

....

....

....

Notes

....

....

....

....

....

....

....

....

....

....

....

....

....

Notes

....

....

....

....

....

....

....

....

....

....

....

....

....

....

Notes

....

....

....

....

....

....

....

....

....

....

....

....

....

....

Notes

···

···

···

···

···

···

···

···

···

···

···

···

···

Notes

Notes

....

....

....

....

....

....

....

....

....

....

....

....

....

Notes

....

....

....

....

....

....

....

....

....

....

....

....

....

....

Notes

....

....

....

....

....

....

....

....

....

....

....

....

....

Notes

Notes

Need More Help?

Do you have more questions about this school? Can't find a certain statistic? College Prowler is here to help. We are the best source of college information on the planet. We have a network of thousands of students who can get the latest information on any school to you ASAP. E-mail us at *info@collegeprowler.com* with your college-related questions. It's like having an older sibling show you the ropes!

Email Us Your College-Related Questions!

Check out **www.collegeprowler.com** for more details.
1.800.290.2682

Notes

....

....

....

....

....

....

....

....

....

....

....

....

....

Tell Us What Life Is Really Like At Your School!

Have you ever wanted to let people know what your school is really like? Now's your chance to help millions of high school students choose the right school.

Let your voice be heard and win cash and prizes!

Check out **www.collegeprowler.com** for more info!

Notes

....

....

....

....

....

....

....

....

....

....

....

....

....

Notes

....

....

....

....

....

....

....

....

....

....

....

....

....

Pros and Cons

Still can't figure out if this is the right school for you?
You've already read through this in-depth guide; why not
list the pros and cons? It will really help with narrowing down
your decision and determining whether or not
this school is right for you.

Pros	Cons

Notes

....

....

....

....

....

....

....

....

....

....

....

....

....

Notes

....

....

....

....

....

....

....

....

....

....

....

....

....

Get Paid To Rep Your City!

Make money for college!

Earn cash by telling your friends about College Prowler!

Excellent Pay + Incentives + Bonuses

Compete with reps across the nation for cash bonuses

Gain marketing and communication skills

Build your resume and gain work experience for future career opportunities

Flexible work hours; make your own schedule

Opportunities for advancement

Contact *sales@collegeprowler.com*
Apply now at **www.collegeprowler.com**

Notes

....

....

....

....

....

....

....

....

....

....

....

....

....

Do You Own A Website?

Would you like to be an affiliate of one of the fastest-growing companies in the publishing industry? Our web affiliates generate a significant income based on customers whom they refer to our website. Start making some cash now! Contact *sales@collegeprowler.com* for more information or call 1.800.290.2682

Apply now at **www.collegeprowler.com**

Notes

....

....

....

....

....

....

....

....

....

....

....

....

....

Notes

Write For Us!
Get Published! Voice Your Opinion.

Writing a College Prowler guidebook is both fun and rewarding; our open-ended format allows your own creativity free reign. Our writers have been featured in national newspapers and have seen their names in bookstores across the country. Now is your chance to break into the publishing industry with one of the country's fastest-growing publishers!

Apply now at **www.collegeprowler.com**

Contact *editor@collegeprowler.com* or
call 1.800.290.2682 for more details.

Notes

....

....

....

....

....

....

....

....

....

....

....

....

....

Notes

....

....

....

....

....

....

....

....

....

....

....

....

....

....

Notes

....

....

....

....

....

....

....

....

....

....

....

....

....

Notes

Notes

Notes

Notes

....

....

....

....

....

....

....

....

....

....

....

....

....